MIRANDA HERNANDEZ

Hack Your Subconscious

Healing with EFT Tapping

First edition

ISBN (print): 979-8-9992975-0-1
ISBN (digital): 979-8-9992975-1-8

This book was professionally typeset on Reedsy.
Find out more at reedsy.com

Contents

Introduction

In the quiet corners of our lives, where whispers of doubt mingle with echoes of past hurts, there exists a profound potential for transformation. This potential is unlocked by the gentle rhythm of fingertips tapping on the body's meridian points. EFT (Emotional Freedom Technique) tapping—an ancient practice that rewrites the scripts of our subconscious minds—offers a powerful path to healing. EFT tapping is a healing tool that combines ancient Chinese acupressure and psychology. It involves tapping with your fingertips on specific meridian points on the body to release emotional and physical tension, restore balance, and promote healing. What makes EFT so compelling is its simplicity and the fact that it can be done anywhere, by anyone.

My name is Miranda, and I stand before you as a witness to the profound impact of EFT tapping on the human spirit. Initially, I was skeptical about this practice. Yet, through serendipitous encounters and personal experiences, I was drawn into the world of EFT tapping—a world where healing is not only possible but inevitable for those who dare to believe.

The purpose of this book is clear: to demystify EFT tapping and make it accessible to all, especially women seeking healing, confidence, and spiritual growth. Through these pages, you will embark on a journey of self-discovery, guided by the principles of EFT tapping, as we navigate the depths of your subconscious mind together.

Here's what you can expect: we'll begin by laying the foundations of EFT tapping, exploring its origins and mechanics, before delving into practical techniques for addressing emotional pain, transforming physical health, and cultivating abundance and success. Along the way, you'll encounter easy-to-follow EFT scripts, personal transformation stories, and scientific evidence supporting the efficacy of EFT tapping. For those ready to take their practice to the next level, we'll explore advanced EFT practices designed to unlock the full potential of your subconscious mind for spiritual growth.

You may wonder about the skeptics—those who question whether tapping on specific points of the body can truly lead to profound shifts in well-being. I understand your skepticism. Yet, I invite you to approach this book with an open heart and mind. Within these pages, you will find not only evidence-based explanations but also personal testimonies from individuals whose lives have been forever changed by this practice.

Above all, this book is about practical application. It's about integrating the principles of EFT tapping into your daily life, creating a ritual of self-care and self-discovery that will guide you toward personal transformation. As you embark on this journey, engage with the material actively, with an open heart and mind. It is through your own efforts and consistency that you will unlock the full potential of EFT tapping. Embrace the transformative power of EFT tapping by making it a part of your daily life, and remember: tap on everything, for every emotion, challenge, or aspiration holds the potential for profound healing and growth.

Let me leave you with this thought: within you lies the power to heal, to grow, and to transform your life in ways you never thought possible. So, take my hand, and together, let us embark on a journey of self-discovery and empowerment—a journey fueled by the transformative power of EFT tapping.

1

Understanding EFT and Your Body

1.1 The Science Behind EFT Tapping: Unraveling How It Works

In the dance between mind and body, EFT tapping emerges as a tool for healing, bridging ancient wisdom and modern science. EFT tapping operates on the principle that the body is a network of energy pathways, known as meridians, through which vital life force flows. By tapping on specific meridian points, we stimulate the body's energy system, restoring balance and harmony.

EFT tapping works by influencing the body's energy system. Each tap sends signals to the brain, activating the relaxation response and promoting a sense of calm and well-being. Through this process, EFT tapping serves as a tool for managing stress and cultivating emotional resilience.

Beyond its physiological effects, EFT tapping interacts with the brain on a psychological level, offering relief from emotional distress and promoting mental health. By engaging with the body's energy system, we tap into the subconscious mind, where deeply ingrained beliefs and emotions reside. The process of tapping helps release trapped emotions and rewire the brain's response to stress, paving the way for emotional healing.

The effectiveness of EFT tapping is supported by a growing body of scientific research and clinical trials. Studies have shown that EFT tapping can reduce symptoms of anxiety, depression, and PTSD, offering a safe and effective alternative to traditional psychological therapies. From improved mood and emotional well-being to enhanced physical health, the benefits of EFT tapping are well-documented.

Unlike traditional psychological therapies that rely on verbal communication, EFT tapping offers a unique approach to healing that integrates both mind and body. While conventional therapies may take weeks or months to yield results, EFT tapping often provides rapid relief from emotional distress and promotes lasting change. By addressing the root cause of emotional issues at the energetic level, EFT tapping offers a holistic approach to healing that transcends the limitations of conventional therapies. Moreover, EFT tapping can complement other health and wellness practices, making it a versatile tool in a holistic healing journey.

The science behind EFT tapping offers a framework for understanding its effects on the mind and body. By tapping into the body's energy system, we unlock the door to healing and transformation, paving the way for a life of greater health, happiness, and vitality.

1.2 Mapping the Meridian Points: Your Body's Healing Pathways

In the dance of energy within the human body, meridian points serve as pathways through which Qi, or life force energy, flows. Rooted in traditional Chinese medicine, these points are crucial in EFT tapping for releasing emotional and physical blockages, promoting holistic healing and well-being. Understanding meridian points is key to harnessing the power of EFT tapping.

Locating Key Points

To engage with EFT tapping, accurately locate and tap on specific meridian points.You can tap on both sides or choose the side you prefer. The acupressure points are symmetrical. Here's a guide to finding each key point:

- **Karate Chop Point:** This is the part of your hand that you would use to deliver a karate chop. Found on both the left and right hands, between the base of the pinky finger and the wrist. This point is associated with the small intestine meridian.
- **Top of the Head (TH):** Locate the crown of your head, you can use all your fingertips to tap on this area. This point, known as the "coronal point."
- **Eyebrow (EB):** Find the beginning of your eyebrow, just above the bridge of your nose. This point is linked to clarity of thought and emotional balance.
- **Side of the Eye (SE):** Continue along the eyebrow to the outer edge of the eye socket, tap on the bone. This point helps process emotions and release stress.

- **Under the Eye (UE):** Move downward to the bone beneath the eye. You can either use the pads of all of your fingers, or just the first two. This point is connected to emotional stability and relaxation.
- **Under the Nose (UN):** Use one hand to locate the area between the nose and upper lip. This point aids in communication and self-expression.
- **Chin (Ch):** Use one hand to find the center of the crease between the bottom lip and chin. This point is linked to grounding and stability.
- **Collarbone (CB):** Locate the notch at the base of your throat and move down about one inch. This point is connected to emotional balance.
- **Under the Arm (UA):** Moving down from the collarbone, find the area approximately four inches below the armpit. This point helps release tension and promote relaxation.

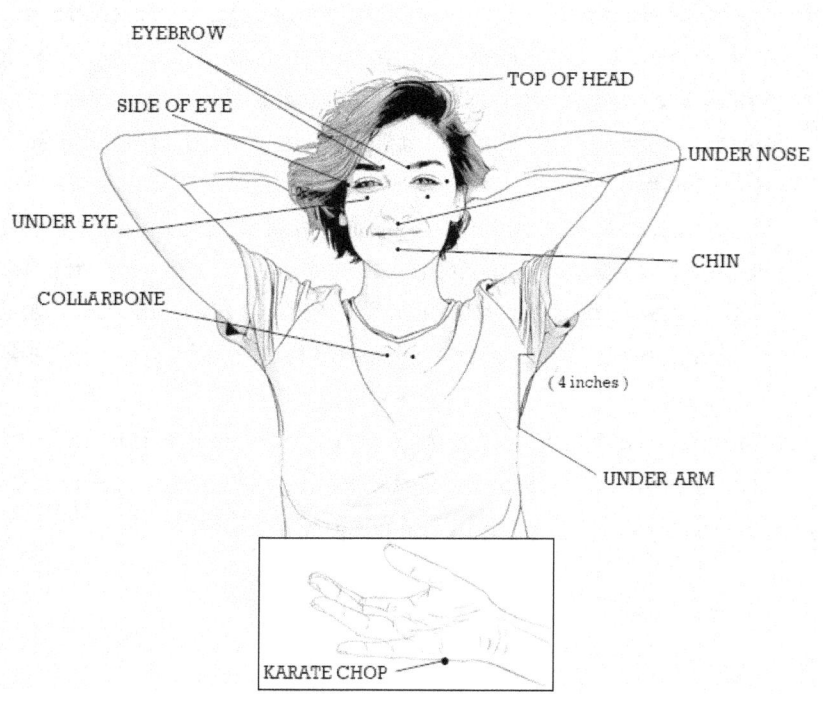

Function of Each Point

Each meridian point corresponds to specific emotions, organs, and bodily functions, influencing our well-being. Understanding these associations can deepen your EFT tapping practice:

- **Karate Chop Point:** Clear any disruptions and promote emotional and physical healing.
- **Top of the Head (TH):** Mental clarity and inspiration.
- **Eyebrow (EB):** Decision-making and emotional stability.
- **Side of the Eye (SE):** Processing emotions and reducing stress.
- **Under the Eye (UE):** Emotional balance and relaxation.

- **Under the Nose (UN):** Clarity of communication and self-expression.
- **Chin (Ch):** Grounding and stability.
- **Collarbone (CB):** Emotional balance and well-being.
- **Under the Arm (UA):** Releasing tension and promoting relaxation.

Strategies for Effective Tapping

To maximize the benefits of EFT tapping, consider these techniques:

- Use gentle yet firm pressure when tapping on each point.
- Tap with the first two fingers of one hand, tap with all fingers of one hand, or use two hands for greater coverage.
- Repeat a short phrase or affirmation while tapping to focus your intention.
- Tap each point multiple times, following a consistent rhythm.
- Pay attention to any sensations or emotions that arise during tapping and allow yourself to fully experience them.

By incorporating these strategies into your EFT tapping practice, you can enhance its effectiveness and promote deeper healing and transformation.

1.3 The Psychology of Healing: EFT's Role in Emotional Wellness

Emotional Processing with EFT

EFT operates on the principle that emotional distress is rooted in disruptions in the body's energy system. By tapping on specific meridian points while focusing on distressing emotions, EFT helps release these blockages and restore balance to the body-mind system. This process facilitates the release of emotional pain and addresses its underlying energetic imbalances. Through EFT, individuals can process deeply held emotions, allowing them to move through unresolved trauma and experience emotional healing.

Building Emotional Resilience

Regular practice of EFT builds emotional resilience over time. By tapping on a range of emotions and issues, individuals strengthen their capacity to cope with stress, adversity, and life's challenges. EFT fosters resilience by providing a safe and structured framework for processing difficult emotions, enhancing self-awareness, and developing healthy coping mechanisms. As individuals continue to practice EFT, they cultivate greater emotional flexibility and adaptability, enabling them to navigate life's ups and downs with more ease.

EFT for Anxiety and Depression

Anxiety and depression, prevalent mental health conditions, significantly impact well-being. EFT offers strategies for managing these symptoms by targeting their emotional roots. By addressing energy disruptions within the body's meridian system and tapping on specific acupressure points while focusing on distressing thoughts, emotions, and physical sensations, EFT restores balance, reducing symptoms.

EFT provides immediate relief from acute anxiety symptoms like racing thoughts and rapid heartbeat by interrupting the body's stress response. Regular practice helps identify and address emotional triggers contributing to chronic symptoms, leading to greater resilience over time. EFT empowers individuals with a tool that can be integrated into daily routines, offering a holistic approach to symptom management and fostering insight and emotional well-being.

Testimonials of Transformation

Experience the impact of EFT through the stories of individuals who have embarked on their journey of emotional healing and growth. These testimonials offer accounts of the transformative power of EFT in promoting emotional wellness, overcoming past traumas, managing anxiety and depression, and reclaiming a sense of joy and vitality. Through their narratives, gain insight into the potential of EFT to facilitate emotional healing and growth, igniting hope and motivation on your own path toward well-being.

Crystal's Story: "When I first started working with EFT, I was overwhelmed by issues in my marriage, weight struggles, and feelings of depression. I realized I had been replaying scenarios without connecting to my feelings. I began tapping on my habit of storytelling, using affirmations like, 'Even though I keep telling these stories, I deeply and completely accept myself.' I focused on my emotions about the drama, uncovering feelings of resentment from always putting others first. Through guided visualization and tapping, I 'uninstalled' the old program of putting others first and 'installed' a new one prioritizing myself. By the weekend, I felt transformed. The alignment of my mind and heart gave me a new perspective, allowing me to feel more grounded and empowered. Today, I'm telling a different, much more positive story about my life."

Mark's Testimonial: *"For as long as I can remember, anxiety and depression have been constant companions in my life, stemming from severe childhood abuse. This led to a challenging journey. However, within just the first week of incorporating tapping into my routine, I've been amazed at the improvement in my sleep. I'm participating in a sleep challenge at night and also adding a tapping session after my morning meditation. Despite my initial skepticism about EFT, which I dismissed as pseudoscience for years, I'm now convinced of its benefits. As a recovery coach, I'm excited to integrate tapping into my practice, recommending it to my clients and incorporating it into daily routines to help them change their relationship with alcohol."*

Vicky's Journey: *"After years of feeling defeated by the loss of my business and working a mind-numbing office job, I discovered a course on EFT tapping. I took the course to heart and literally tapped on everything. Initially, nothing changed, but as I persisted, I experienced profound shifts. Tapping helped me confront my fears, build confidence, and believe in my ability to start a new business. It also transformed my relationships, allowing me to set healthy boundaries and heal old wounds. I found a passion for songwriting, reconnected with family, and achieved financial success beyond my dreams, earning more in a month than I previously did in a year. Now, I live a life of abundance, joy, and fulfillment, grateful for the impact of tapping."*

Dan's Journey: *"My significant breakthrough came when I used an EFT session on healing colds and respiratory issues, incorporating Louise Hay's affirmations. On Monday, I developed a severe cold with major breathing problems. I initially tried various tapping techniques focused on healing, but on Wednesday, I discovered this particular session. The turnaround has been astonishing! After each session, my breathing improved dramatically, and I now feel so much better. It also surfaced a lot of old family issues, and I'm grateful to be releasing those as well."*

1.4 EFT and stress management: A Neuroscientific Perspective

Stress Response in the Brain

Understanding the relationship between stress and the brain is essential in comprehending the effectiveness of EFT in stress management. The amygdala, the part of the brain responsible for the stress response, triggers the fight-or-flight mode in reaction to perceived threats. In modern life, this survival instinct is often overstimulated, leading to chronic stress and anxiety. EFT tapping helps by sending calming signals to the brain while focusing on distressing emotions or physical sensations, allowing it to relax and reducing the overall stress response.

Neuroplasticity and EFT

Neuroplasticity, the brain's ability to reorganize and form new neural connections, plays a crucial role in stress management and emotional regulation. EFT tapping promotes neuroplasticity by engaging the brain in repetitive sensory stimulation through tapping on meridian points. This stimulation encourages the brain to rewire neural pathways associated with stress, anxiety, and negative emotions, leading to long-term changes in how the brain processes and responds to stressors.

Cortisol Reduction

Cortisol, often referred to as the stress hormone, is released in response to stress and plays a central role in the body's physiological stress response. Elevated cortisol levels over prolonged periods can have detrimental effects on health, contributing to a range of physical and mental health issues. Research has demonstrated the efficacy of EFT in reducing cortisol levels. Dr. Dawson Church's 2012 study found that EFT led to a 24% reduction in cortisol levels, and a 2020 study replicated these results with a 43% reduction after just one hour of tapping. By incorporating EFT tapping into daily practice, individuals can regulate cortisol levels and promote overall well-being.

Practical Stress-Reduction Techniques

Empowering individuals with practical stress-reduction techniques enhances overall resilience and well-being. EFT offers a simple tool for managing stress in everyday life. Below are EFT tapping script routines designed for quick stress relief:

- **The Calming Cascade:** Tap gently on the top of your head, the inside of your eyebrows, the side of your eye, under your eye, under your nose, on your chin, on your collarbone, and under your arm while repeating calming affirmations such as "I am calm and centered" or "I release stress and tension from my body."
- **The Grounding Gratitude:** Tap on the top of your head, your temples, your cheeks, your chest, your stomach, and your wrists while focusing on feelings of gratitude and appreciation. Take deep breaths and visualize yourself grounded and connected to the present moment.

1.5 Balancing Your Energy Flow: The Key to Harmonious Living

Understanding Energy Balance

Central to the practice of EFT is the concept of energy balance, which refers to the harmonious flow of energy throughout the body. Energy balance is vital for well-being, as disruptions or blockages in the body's energy system can manifest as physical, mental, and emotional issues. Introducing this concept lays the foundation for understanding the importance of EFT in restoring and maintaining energy balance for health and vitality.

EFT's Role in Energy Regulation

EFT serves as a tool for energy regulation, helping to rebalance and harmonize the body's energy system. By tapping on specific meridian points while focusing on distressing emotions or physical symptoms, EFT helps release blocked energy and restore the smooth flow of energy throughout the body. This process promotes physical healing and enhances mental clarity, emotional stability, and overall vitality.

Daily Practices for Energy Balance

Empowering yourself with practical daily EFT routines is essential for promoting balanced energy flow. Here are some examples of daily EFT practices to incorporate into your routine:

- **Morning Energy Boost:** Begin your day with a quick EFT tapping session to energize your body and mind. Focus on tapping on key meridian points while repeating affirmations of energy and vitality, such as "I am filled with vibrant energy" or "I welcome the flow of positive energy into my life."

- **Midday Stress Release:** Take a few minutes during your lunch break or whenever you feel stressed to practice EFT tapping. Address any tension or anxiety by tapping on meridian points and acknowledging your feelings. Allow yourself to release stress with each tap, breathing deeply and letting go of negativity.
- **Evening Relaxation Routine:** Wind down at the end of the day with a soothing EFT tapping session to promote relaxation and restful sleep. Focus on tapping on meridian points while affirming feelings of peace and tranquility, such as "I release the day's stress and embrace relaxation" or "I am calm and at ease."

For detailed tapping scripts for these EFT practices, refer to the section titled "EFT Scripts: Transformative Tapping for Every Journey" at the back of this book, and remember to customize the scripts provided in this section to suit your unique needs and goals with words and phrasing that resonate with you.

Signs of Improved Energy Flow

As you incorporate EFT into your daily routine and experience improved energy flow, you may notice changes in your mental, emotional, and physical states. These changes may include increased feelings of vitality and well-being, reduced stress and anxiety, improved mood and emotional stability, enhanced mental clarity and focus, and greater resilience to life's challenges. By observing these signs, you can gain confidence in the effectiveness of EFT in promoting balanced energy flow and harmonious living.

2

Preparing for Your EFT Journey

2.1 Setting Intentions for Healing: The Power of Your Mindset

In the journey of EFT, mindset plays a pivotal role, acting as the compass guiding us through our emotions and experiences. By setting clear intentions, we harness the power of our subconscious mind to steer us towards healing and transformation.

The Importance of Intentions

Intentions serve as the cornerstone of our EFT practice, shaping the direction of our healing journey. They provide clarity, focus, and purpose, acting as beacons in times of darkness. When we set clear intentions, we signal our commitment to growth and healing, opening ourselves to receive life's abundance.

Crafting Your Healing Intentions

Crafting healing intentions is a personal process, rooted in self-awareness and introspection. Reflect on areas of your life where you seek healing and transformation. Are there emotional wounds that need to be healed? Goals you wish to achieve? Relationships you long to mend? Formulate your intentions with clarity and specificity, infusing them with positive energy and sincerity.

Aligning Intentions with Actions

Intentions without action are merely wishes. To manifest our desires, we must align our daily actions with our intentions. This means making conscious choices that support our healing journey, whether it's setting aside time for regular tapping sessions, practicing self-care, or engaging in activities that nourish our soul. By taking consistent and intentional action, we pave the way for healing and growth.

Visualization Techniques

Visualization is a tool that can amplify the effects of intention-setting. Through visualization, we imagine ourselves embodying our desired outcomes, creating a mental blueprint for success. Whether it's visualizing ourselves free from pain, achieving our goals, or experiencing inner peace, visualization enhances our emotional state, making our intentions more tangible and achievable.

Incorporate visualization into your EFT practice by taking a few moments each day to close your eyes and visualize yourself living your intentions. See yourself bathed in the light of healing, surrounded by love and abundance. Allow yourself to feel the emotions associated with your intentions, anchoring them into your subconscious mind.

By integrating these practices into your daily routine, you can harness the full potential of EFT tapping, transforming your mindset and paving the way for lasting healing and growth.

2.2 Creating Your Personal EFT Space: Tips for a Conducive Environment

In the practice of EFT, the environment plays a crucial role in fostering safety, comfort, and receptivity. By creating a personal EFT space, we cultivate a sanctuary for healing, allowing us to explore our emotions and experiences with greater ease and clarity.

Begin by carving out a dedicated space in your home or workspace for your EFT practice. This space should evoke tranquility and serenity, free from distractions and noise. Consider elements such as soft lighting, comfortable seating, crystals, and soothing decor to create a nurturing environment conducive to relaxation and emotional release.

Incorporate rituals into your tapping practice to imbue it with a sense of sacredness and intentionality. Begin each session by lighting a candle or incense, creating a space with LED lighting, smudging with sage, or setting an intention for healing and transformation. Create a routine that signals to your mind and body that it's time for deep inner work and self-discovery.

Consider environmental factors that can influence your EFT sessions. Ensure that your space is free from harsh lighting or loud noises that may disrupt your focus. Experiment with soothing sounds like nature sounds, binaural beats, solfeggio frequencies, or gentle music to create a calming atmosphere. Consider using aromatherapy with essential oils known for their relaxation and grounding properties, such as lavender or chamomile.

While having a dedicated EFT space can enhance your practice, remember that EFT is a versatile tool that can be accessed anywhere. Whether you're at home, at work, or on the go, you can incorporate tapping into your daily routine. Build routines that fit your lifestyle, and remember that the true power of EFT lies in its adaptability and accessibility.

2.3 Understanding Your Healing Timeline: Setting Realistic Expectations

Embarking on an EFT journey is a personal and transformative experience, unique to each individual. As you prepare to dive into this practice, it's essential to set realistic expectations for your healing journey, understanding that healing is not linear but a dynamic process of growth and evolution.

Every person's healing journey is as unique as their fingerprint, shaped by factors including past experiences, emotional resilience, and current life circumstances. What works for one person may not work for another, and it's important to honor and respect the individuality of each path to healing.

Typical Progression with EFT

While the healing journey is highly individualized, there are common patterns and milestones that newcomers to EFT may encounter. Initially, many individuals experience a sense of relief and lightness as they begin to tap into and release pent-up emotions and energy. As the practice deepens, layers of emotional and physical tension may gradually unravel, paving the way for profound insights and breakthroughs.

Patience and persistence are indispensable allies on the path to healing with EFT. It's essential to cultivate a mindset of patience, understanding that healing takes time and cannot be rushed. Setbacks and challenges may arise along the way, but it's through perseverance and dedication that true transformation occurs.

As you progress on your healing journey, your needs and priorities may shift, requiring adjustments to your EFT practice. Remain open and flexible, attuning to your body's signals and intuition to guide you in modifying your tapping techniques and approaches. Embrace the process of evolution and growth, trusting that each step forward brings you closer to a state of wholeness and well-being.

By setting realistic expectations, exercising patience and persistence, and remaining adaptable to change, you empower yourself to navigate your healing journey with grace, resilience, and self-discovery.

2.4 Personalizing Your EFT Practice: Tailoring Techniques to Fit Your Life

Embracing EFT is not just about following a set of prescribed steps; it's about making the practice your own, integrating it seamlessly into your unique life journey. Personalizing your EFT practice allows you to harness its transformative power in a way that resonates deeply with your individual needs, beliefs, and values.

One of the beauties of EFT is its adaptability to address a wide range of issues and goals. Empower yourself by learning how to modify tapping scripts to suit your specific challenges and aspirations. Whether it's tweaking the language to better reflect your emotions or tailoring the tapping script to target particular acupressure points, customization allows you to personalize your healing journey.

Infuse your EFT practice with your personal beliefs and values to deepen its impact and resonance. Consider how your core values align with your healing intentions, and integrate affirmations and visualizations that resonate with your spiritual or philosophical beliefs. By weaving these elements into your practice, you create a powerful synergy between mind, body, and spirit.

EFT in Daily Life

EFT isn't confined to designated tapping sessions; it's a versatile tool that can be integrated into various aspects of daily life. Explore ways to incorporate tapping into your morning routine to set a positive tone for the day ahead, or use it as a tool for managing stress and anxiety during challenging moments. By weaving EFT into your daily rituals, you infuse each moment with mindfulness and intentionality.

Feedback Loops

Embrace the practice of creating feedback loops to continually refine and enhance your personal EFT practice. Pay attention to how your body and emotions respond to different tapping techniques, and use this feedback to adjust and fine-tune your approach over time. By remaining open to learning and growth, you empower yourself to deepen your connection with EFT and maximize its potential for healing and transformation.

As you personalize your EFT practice, remember that there is no one-size-fits-all approach. Trust your intuition, honor your unique journey, and allow yourself the freedom to explore and experiment with different techniques and modalities. In doing so, you cultivate a practice that is not only deeply effective but also authentically yours.

Creating Custom EFT Tapping Scripts: A Comprehensive Guide

Crafting your own EFT tapping scripts allows you to address your unique needs, goals, and experiences. This personalized approach enhances the effectiveness of EFT, making it a versatile tool for emotional and spiritual growth. Here's a step-by-step guide to help you structure your tapping scripts:

Step 1: Identify the Issue or Goal

Begin by clearly identifying the specific issue or goal you want to address. This could be an emotional challenge, a physical symptom, a limiting belief, or a spiritual aspiration. Write down a concise statement of your issue or goal.

Example:

Issue: "I feel anxious about public speaking."

Goal: "I want to feel confident and calm when speaking in public."

Step 2: Assess the Emotional Intensity

Evaluate the intensity of your feelings related to the issue on a scale of 0 to 10, with 0 being no intensity and 10 being the highest. This step helps track progress and gauge the effectiveness of your tapping.

Example:

Emotional Intensity: 7

Step 3: Craft the Setup Statement

The setup statement acknowledges the issue while affirming self-acceptance. It typically follows this structure:

"Even though [describe the issue], I deeply and completely accept myself."

Example:

"Even though I feel anxious about public speaking, I deeply and completely accept myself."

Step 4: Develop the Reminder Phrases

Reminder phrases are short, focused phrases that encapsulate the issue and are used at each tapping point. These phrases help maintain focus on the issue as you tap through the points.

Example:

"This public speaking anxiety."

Step 5: Create Positive Affirmations

Incorporate positive affirmations to shift your mindset and reinforce desired outcomes. These can be included after a few rounds of tapping on the negative aspects.

Example:
"I am becoming more confident and calm when speaking in public."

Step 6: Structure the Tapping Script

Combine the setup statement, reminder phrases, and positive affirmations into a cohesive script. Here's a template you can follow:

Setup Statement (repeat 3 times while tapping on the Karate Chop point):

"Even though [describe the issue], I deeply and completely accept myself."

Tapping Script (tap on each point while repeating the reminder phrase):

- Eyebrow (EB): "[Issue]"
- Side of Eye (SE): "[Issue]"
- Under Eye (UE): "[Issue]"
- Under Nose (UN): "[Issue]"
- Chin (CH): "[Issue]"
- Collarbone (CB): "[Issue]"
- Under Arm (UA): "[Issue]"
- Top of Head (TH): "[Issue]"

Positive Affirmations (tap on each point while repeating positive statements):

- Eyebrow (EB): "[Positive outcome]"
- Side of Eye (SE): "[Positive outcome]"
- Under Eye (UE): "[Positive outcome]"
- Under Nose (UN): "[Positive outcome]"
- Chin (CH): "[Positive outcome]"
- Collarbone (CB): "[Positive outcome]"

- Under Arm (UA): "[Positive outcome]"
- Top of Head (TH): "[Positive outcome]"

Example Custom Script: Public Speaking Anxiety

Setup Statement: "Even though I feel anxious about public speaking, I deeply and completely accept myself." (Repeat 3 times)

Tapping Script:

- EB: "This public speaking anxiety."
- SE: "This anxiety in my body."
- UE: "I feel nervous and scared."
- UN: "This fear of judgment."
- CH: "This anxiety about speaking."
- CB: "I feel it in my chest."
- UA: "This public speaking anxiety."
- TH: "I feel anxious."

Positive Affirmations:

- EB: "I am becoming more confident."
- SE: "I can speak calmly."
- UE: "I feel more at ease."
- UN: "I trust my abilities."
- CH: "I am confident."
- CB: "I am calm and composed."
- UA: "I enjoy speaking in public."
- TH: "I am confident and calm."

Step 7: Review and Refine

After completing the tapping script, reassess the emotional intensity. If it's still high, repeat the process until you notice a significant reduction in intensity. Feel free to adjust the script as needed to better fit your evolving feelings and insights.

Tips for Effective Script Creation

- **Be Specific:** The more specific you are about the issue, the more effective the tapping will be.
- **Tune Into Your Emotions:** Pay attention to your feelings and physical sensations as you tap. Modify your script based on what arises.
- **Incorporate Visualization:** Visualize positive outcomes while tapping to reinforce the desired changes.
- **Practice Regularly:** Consistent practice helps reinforce new beliefs and behaviors.

By following this guide, you can create personalized EFT tapping scripts that effectively address your unique needs and goals, enhancing your emotional and spiritual well-being.

2.5 Overcoming Skepticism: Building Trust in EFT Methods

Skepticism around EFT often stems from misunderstandings or lack of awareness about the substantial body of evidence supporting its efficacy. This section addresses common skepticisms and provides counter arguments grounded in scientific evidence and testimonials from individuals who have experienced its benefits firsthand.

EFT Lacks Scientific Validity

While EFT was initially met with skepticism, numerous studies have demonstrated its efficacy in reducing stress, anxiety, and various forms of psychological distress. For example, a study published in the "Journal of Nervous and Mental Disease" found that EFT significantly reduced anxiety and stress in participants compared to those who received no treatment. Furthermore, research in the "Journal of Traumatic Stress" reported that EFT effectively reduced symptoms of PTSD in veterans, showcasing its potential for addressing severe psychological conditions.

EFT Relies on Placebo Effect

Critics often attribute the benefits of EFT to the placebo effect rather than its actual mechanisms. However, studies utilizing control groups and randomized trials have consistently shown that EFT produces effects beyond those of a placebo. Brain imaging studies have provided insights into the neurobiological mechanisms underlying EFT, further validating its efficacy as a therapeutic technique.

Clinical Studies

Numerous clinical studies have highlighted EFT's effectiveness. For instance, the study published in the "Journal of Nervous and Mental Disease" confirmed that EFT significantly reduces anxiety and stress levels. Additionally, a study focusing on veterans with PTSD found that after six EFT treatment sessions, 90% of participants no longer met the clinical criteria for PTSD, and these results were replicated in further studies, demonstrating consistent positive outcomes.

Meta-Analyses

Meta-analyses, which review and synthesize data from multiple studies, have confirmed EFT's effectiveness. These analyses indicate that EFT is more than just a fad, providing robust evidence of its therapeutic benefits. For example, a meta-analysis published in "Frontiers in Psychology" reviewed several randomized controlled trials (RCTs) and found that EFT significantly reduced PTSD symptoms, anxiety, and other psychological distress, further solidifying its evidence-based practice status.

Anecdotal Evidence Is Not Sufficient

While anecdotal evidence alone may not suffice, the abundance of personal testimonials from individuals who have experienced profound transformations through EFT cannot be discounted. These firsthand accounts, coupled with empirical research, paint a compelling picture of EFT's potential for healing and personal growth. Hearing stories of real people overcoming trauma, phobias, and chronic pain through EFT can inspire hope and encourage skeptics to explore its benefits further.

Here are some testimonials from individuals who have experienced the benefits of EFT firsthand:

Jane's Story: Finding Relief from Everyday Challenges

"I was initially skeptical, but after reading the reviews and research, I decided to give EFT a try. It has been transformative for me and my family. Whether dealing with minor issues or deep traumas, tapping has provided us with a simple, cost-free tool to manage and overcome a variety of problems. If you're looking for a boost of energy, relief from pain, or an uplift in mood, I encourage you to suspend disbelief and try EFT. It has truly made a difference for us." - Jane

Kim's Journey: Overcoming Chronic Pain

"After months of shoulder pain and poor sleep, I was desperate for relief. Medical treatments weren't helping, so I decided to try EFT. By committing to regular tapping sessions, I saw my pain decrease from a 10 to a 3. With more focused sessions on feelings of being unsupported, my pain eventually dropped to a 0. I can't express how grateful I am for EFT. It has been a lifesaver." - Kim

Norman's Testimony: Healing from PTSD

"I learned about EFT a year ago but only started using it consistently last month. As a veteran with PTSD and other issues, tapping has been a godsend. It has helped me resolve many of my challenges, providing a level of relief I hadn't found with other treatments. EFT has become an essential tool in my healing journey." - Norman

These testimonials offer a glimpse into the transformative power of EFT and the profound impact it can have on individuals' lives.

Personal Experimentation

Approach EFT with an open mind. Instead of relying solely on others' experiences, engage in personal experimentation. Try out different tapping scripts and observe how they affect your emotional and physical well-being. You can create custom tapping scripts or find scripts in books, online, on social media, on YouTube, or apps like The Tapping Solution.

Connecting with the EFT Community

Connecting with others who are practicing EFT can be helpful. Join online forums, find a practitioner, attend workshops, or find local meetups. Connecting with the broader EFT community can provide support, guidance, and shared learning experiences.

Tracking Progress

Consider documenting your EFT journey to visually represent the benefits over time. Keep a journal to record your tapping sessions, noting any changes in your emotional state or physical symptoms, and reflecting on your progress regularly. Tracking your progress can help you build trust in the efficacy of EFT methods and reinforce your commitment to the practice.

Invitation for Personal Research

Conduct your own research into the scientific evidence and success stories surrounding EFT. Exploring a variety of sources can provide you with a deeper understanding of its potential and efficacy. By staying informed and engaged, you can make the most of your EFT journey and discover the profound benefits it can offer.

2.6 Integrating EFT into Your Daily Routine: Making It Stick

Incorporating EFT into your daily life is key to reaping its benefits consistently. Here's how to seamlessly integrate tapping into your routine:

Habit Formation with EFT

Dive into the psychology of habit formation. Learn how to harness the power of repetition and consistency to make EFT a natural part of your daily ritual. By understanding the science behind habit formation, you can cultivate a sustainable tapping practice. Start by setting a specific time each day for your EFT sessions, whether it's first thing in the morning, during lunch breaks, or before bed. Consistency is key, so choose a time that fits naturally into your daily schedule.

EFT Tapping Mini-Sessions

Explore the concept of mini-sessions—short, focused tapping routines that you can do anytime, anywhere. These bite-sized sessions are perfect for busy schedules and can target specific issues or emotions as they arise throughout the day. For example, if you feel a surge of anxiety before a meeting, take a few moments to do a quick tapping session to calm your nerves. The flexibility of mini-sessions allows you to integrate EFT seamlessly into your daily life, addressing emotional and physical needs as they come up.

Reminder Systems

Discover effective strategies for setting up reminders and prompts to ensure regular EFT practice. Whether it's setting alarms on your phone, leaving sticky notes in visible places, or integrating tapping into existing routines, find what works best for you to keep tapping on your radar. Some people find it helpful to pair tapping with another daily habit, like brushing their teeth or making their morning coffee. This pairing can serve as a natural reminder and make it easier to incorporate tapping into your routine.

Celebrating Milestones

Emphasize the importance of acknowledging and celebrating your progress along the EFT journey. Recognizing milestones, no matter how small, can boost motivation and reinforce the habit of tapping. Whether it's reaching a goal, overcoming a challenge, or simply committing to regular practice, take the time to celebrate your achievements and keep the momentum going. Consider keeping a journal to track your progress and reflect on how far you've come. This practice not only provides motivation but also helps you see the tangible benefits of EFT over time.

By integrating these strategies into your daily routine, you can ensure that EFT becomes a lasting and effective part of your life, supporting your journey towards emotional and physical well-being.

3

Tapping Techniques for Beginners

3.1 Basic Tapping Sequence: A Step-by-Guide

In embarking on your journey with EFT, let's start with the foundational practice: the basic tapping sequence. EFT is wonderfully accessible, and this step-by-step guide ensures you're tapping into its transformative potential with ease.

Sequential Overview

Begin by grounding yourself. Find a comfortable position and take a few deep breaths to center your awareness. Now, let's dive into the sequential walk through of the basic EFT tapping sequence.

Point-by-Point Instructions:

- **Karate Chop Point:** With your fingertips, gently tap on the karate chop point on the side of your hand. Repeat a setup phrase or affirmation to tune into your intention for tapping.
- Example Setup Phrase: "Even though I feel anxious, I deeply and completely accept myself."
- **Eyebrow Point:** Moving to the inside of your eyebrow, tap gently with two or three fingers. Follow the brow bone from the bridge of your nose outwards.
- Example Reminder Phrase: "This anxiety."
- **Side of Eye Point:** Keep tapping with two or three fingers, tap on the outer edge of your eye socket near the temples. Maintain a gentle tapping pressure, focusing on the sensation.
- Example Reminder Phrase: "This tension."
- **Under Eye Point:** Shift your tapping underneath the eye along the bone of the eye socket. Feel the connection between your fingertips and your body.
- Example Reminder Phrase: "This stress."
- **Under Nose Point:** Direct your tapping to the area between your nose and upper lip with three fingers of one hand. Tune into the rhythm of your breath as you tap.
- Example Reminder Phrase: "These worries."
- **Chin Point:** Move to the indentation between your chin and lower lip and keep tapping with three fingers of one hand. Let your tapping be a gentle reminder of your presence in this moment.
- Example Reminder Phrase: "This fear."
- **Collarbone Point:** Tap where your collarbone meets your sternum, you can either use the pads of your fingers, as you've tapped on other points, or use your whole hand. Notice any sensations that arise with each tap.

- Example Reminder Phrase: "This anxiety."
- **Under Arm Point:** Use your whole hand to tap on the side of your body, approximately four inches below your armpit. Connect with the soothing rhythm of your breath as you tap here.
- Example Reminder Phrase: "This stress."
- **Top of Head Point:** Finally, tap gently on the crown of your head with the fingertips of one or both hands. Feel the connection with your entire body as you tap, allowing any remaining tension to release.
- Example Reminder Phrase: "This remaining anxiety."

Breathing Techniques

As you tap through each point, remember to synchronize your breath. Inhale deeply through your nose, allowing the breath to expand your belly, and exhale slowly through your mouth, releasing any tension or resistance.

Common Mistakes to Avoid

Stay mindful of common pitfalls. Ensure your tapping pressure is gentle yet firm, avoiding excessive force. Stay present with your emotions and sensations, allowing them to guide you through the tapping process.

With this step-by-step guide, you're equipped to embark on your journey with EFT, tapping into your inner wellspring of healing and resilience with confidence and grace.

3.2 Crafting Effective Affirmations: The Heart of Your Tapping Practice

In this section, we explore the transformative potential of affirmations within EFT. Crafting personalized affirmations is a key aspect of your tapping practice, empowering you to harness positive language to reprogram your subconscious mind and facilitate healing and growth.

The Power of Positive Affirmations

Affirmations are tools for reshaping our inner dialogue and beliefs. By consciously choosing positive, empowering statements, we can override limiting beliefs and cultivate a mindset of abundance, resilience, and self-compassion. Affirmations act as seeds planted in the fertile soil of our subconscious, blossoming into new thought patterns and behaviors over time.

To create your personalized affirmations, start by reflecting on areas of your life where you seek transformation and healing. Identify any negative self-talk or limiting beliefs that may be holding you back. Then, reframe these beliefs into positive affirmations that align with your desired outcomes and aspirations. Remember, affirmations should be present tense, positive, and specific, resonating deeply with your authentic self.

Incorporating Affirmations into Tapping

Once you've crafted your affirmations, integrate them into your EFT tapping routine. Begin each tapping session by reciting your chosen affirmations aloud or silently, anchoring them in your mind and heart.

As you tap on each meridian point, infuse your affirmations with intention and conviction, allowing them to penetrate deep into your subconscious mind.

Examples of Affirmations for Various Issues:

To guide you in this process, here are some examples of affirmations tailored to common emotional and physical issues:

- **Emotional Healing:** "I release all past pain and embrace love and joy in my life."
- **Self-Confidence:** "I am worthy of love and respect, exactly as I am."
- **Physical Well-Being:** "My body is strong, healthy, and vibrant, radiating vitality and energy."
- **Abundance:** "I attract abundance and prosperity into my life effortlessly and joyfully."
- **Inner Peace:** "I am calm, centered, and at peace, regardless of external circumstances."

These affirmations serve as guides on your journey of self-discovery and empowerment, illuminating the path towards wholeness and fulfillment. By infusing your tapping practice with affirmations, you unlock the door to a life filled with possibilities and joy.

By weaving these elements into your practice, you create a powerful synergy between mind, body, and spirit, enhancing the effectiveness of your EFT practice and fostering a deeper sense of connection and healing.

3.3 Navigating Emotional Release: Safe Practices for Beginners

Embarking on your tapping journey, it's crucial to navigate the terrain of emotional release with care and compassion. Here, we delve into safe practices for beginners to traverse this transformative process.

Recognizing Emotional Release

As you engage in tapping, attune yourself to the subtle shifts within your being. Recognize the signs of emotional release—perhaps tears, sighs, or a sense of lightness—as indications of the healing unfolding within. These signs are natural and affirm that your tapping practice is effectively addressing and releasing stored emotional energy.

Managing Intense Emotions

If you encounter intense emotions during tapping, remember that you are safe and supported. Offer yourself gentle reassurance and use grounding techniques such as deep breathing or affirmations to anchor yourself in the present moment. Techniques like placing your hand on your heart, feeling your feet on the ground, or visualizing a place of safety can help stabilize your emotions.

Creating a Support System

Having a support system in place, whether friends, family, or a trusted therapist, underscores the importance of community in your healing journey. Cultivate a network of understanding individuals who can offer compassion and encouragement when navigating deep emotional waters. Sharing your experiences with someone you trust can provide additional perspectives and emotional support.

Self-Care Post-Tapping

After tapping sessions involving significant emotional release, prioritize self-care to honor the vulnerability and courage within you. Engage in nurturing activities such as journaling, taking a soothing bath, or spending time in nature to replenish your spirit and integrate the insights gained from your tapping practice. Allow yourself time to rest and reflect, acknowledging the progress you are making on your healing journey.

Integration of Practice

To further support your emotional well-being, integrate regular tapping sessions into your routine. Consistency in practice helps process emotions gradually and gently. Approach each session with curiosity and kindness towards yourself, celebrating even small steps forward.

By embracing these practices, you ensure that your journey through emotional release with EFT tapping is both safe and healing. Remember, this is a personal journey, and it's important to go at your own pace, honoring your unique process and needs.

3.4 Quick Stress-Relief Tapping for Busy Schedules

In the hustle and bustle of modern life, finding moments of calm amidst chaos is essential. Here, we present a swift and effective tapping routine tailored for busy schedules, ensuring stress relief is always within reach.

Five-Minute Tapping Routine

Introducing a concise yet potent tapping script, this five-minute routine offers a sanctuary of serenity in the midst of your bustling day. With focused intention and gentle taps, you can swiftly alleviate stress and reclaim a sense of inner peace.

1. **Setup Statement:** While tapping on the Karate Chop point, repeat: "Even though I feel stressed, I deeply and completely accept myself."
2. **Eyebrow Point:** "I'm feeling stressed"
3. **Side of the Eye:** "It's overwhelming"
4. **Under Eye:** "This stress in my body"
5. **Under Nose:** "I feel tense"
6. **Chin Point:** "This stress is weighing me down"
7. **Collarbone Point:** "I release this stress"
8. **Under Arm:** "Letting go of tension"
9. **Top of Head:** "I am calm and relaxed"

Repeat this script as needed until you feel a sense of relief and relaxation.

Tapping on the Go

Discover the art of discreet tapping, a valuable skill for managing stress in any setting. Learn simple and effective techniques to tap inconspicuously on key meridian points, ensuring stress relief is always at your fingertips.

- **Finger Tapping:** Master the subtle art of finger tapping. Lightly tap on each point with your index and middle fingers while maintaining a relaxed hand position, blending tapping into your everyday movements.

- **Butterfly Hug:** Embrace the butterfly hug. Cross your arms over your chest and tap gently on your collar bones with your fingertips. Take slow, deep breaths as you tap, creating a soothing rhythm that calms both body and mind.
- **Palm Tapping:** Practice palm tapping. Tap the palm of one hand with the fingertips of the other, alternating between hands as you move through the points. This method allows you to tap unnoticed, perfect for situations where privacy is limited.
- **Stealth Tapping:** Master stealth tapping for maximum discretion. Tap on the points with your fingertips while incorporating subtle movements, such as adjusting your hair or glasses, to conceal the tapping action. With practice, you can integrate tapping into your daily routine, enjoying stress relief wherever you go.

Emergency Tapping Techniques

In times of sudden stress or panic, having effective tapping techniques at your fingertips can make all the difference. Explore these simple yet powerful routines crafted to diffuse tension and restore equilibrium in moments of need.

1. **Calm Amidst Chaos:** Begin by tapping on the karate chop point while repeating a calming affirmation, such as "Even though I feel overwhelmed, I deeply and completely accept myself." Then, tap on each of the other points, focusing on releasing tension and restoring calm. Repeat the routine as needed until you feel centered and grounded.

2. **Breathing Ease:** Focus on your breath as you tap on the eyebrow

point, side of the eye, and under the nose, taking slow, deep breaths with each tap. Visualize inhaling calm and exhaling tension as you move through the points. Continue tapping until you feel a sense of ease and relaxation wash over you.

3. **Instant Relief:** Tap rapidly on the collarbone point while repeating a soothing mantra, such as "I am safe, I am calm." This rapid tapping technique helps to quickly shift your focus away from the source of stress and restore a sense of balance and control. Repeat as necessary until you feel tension melting away.

4. **Grounding Exercise:** Tap on the top of your head, back of the head, and under the arm points while visualizing roots extending from your feet into the earth. With each tap, imagine yourself becoming more grounded and rooted in the present moment. This grounding exercise helps to anchor you during moments of overwhelm and uncertainty.

5. **Heart Centered Healing:** Place one hand over your heart and tap gently with the other hand on the heart center point. Close your eyes and breathe deeply as you tap, allowing feelings of love and compassion to flow through you. This heart-centered tapping helps to soothe the nervous system and restore a sense of inner peace and balance.

Integrating Tapping with Other Stress-Relief Methods

Unlock the potential of combining tapping with other stress-relief modalities. Explore how integrating EFT with practices such as mindfulness, deep breathing, or aromatherapy amplifies tranquility and well-being, offering a holistic approach to stress management. Experiment with combining tapping with other techniques to enhance its effectiveness. Begin your stress-relief routine with a few minutes of deep breathing or mindfulness meditation to center yourself, then transition into tapping to further release tension and promote relaxation. Alternatively, incorporate aromatherapy by diffusing calming essential oils such as lavender or chamomile while tapping to create a soothing multisensory experience.

3.5 Tapping Away Physical Discomfort: Headaches and Tension Relief

Ease the burden of physical discomfort with targeted tapping scripts designed to alleviate headaches, muscle tension, and stiffness. Discover the power of EFT in listening to your body and employing preventative measures to foster long-term relief and well-being.

EFT for Headaches

Combat headaches and migraines with a specialized tapping script crafted to ease discomfort and restore balance. Begin by tapping on the eyebrow point, side of the eye, and under the eye while focusing on releasing tension and promoting relaxation. Continue tapping on each meridian point, addressing the specific areas of discomfort, and affirming your body's ability to find relief.

Setup Statement: While tapping on the Karate Chop point, repeat: "Even though I have this headache, I deeply and completely accept myself."
Tapping Script:

- Eyebrow: "This headache"
- Side of Eye: "This pain in my head"

- Under Eye: "I release this tension"
- Under Nose: "This discomfort"
- Chin: "I allow my head to relax"
- Collarbone: "This headache is easing"
- Under Arm: "Releasing this pain"
- Top of Head: "My head is feeling better"

Tapping for Muscle Tension

Address muscle tension and stiffness with targeted tapping techniques designed to promote relaxation and ease discomfort. Tap on the collarbone point, under the arm, and top of the head, while focusing on releasing tension and restoring flexibility to tight muscles. With each tap, visualize the muscles softening and becoming more pliable, allowing for greater freedom of movement and comfort.

Setup Statement: While tapping on the Karate Chop point, repeat: "Even though I have this muscle tension, I deeply and completely accept myself."
Tapping Script:

- Eyebrow: "This muscle tension"
- Side of Eye: "These tight muscles"
- Under Eye: "I release this stiffness"
- Under Nose: "This discomfort in my body"
- Chin: "My muscles are relaxing"
- Collarbone: "This tension is easing"
- Under Arm: "Releasing this tightness"
- Top of Head: "My body is feeling more relaxed"

Listening to Your Body

Develop a deeper connection with your body by tuning into bodily sensations and responding with tailored tapping approaches. Pay attention to areas of tension or discomfort, and adjust your tapping script accordingly to address the specific needs of your body. By listening to your body's cues and responding with compassion and care, you can effectively alleviate physical discomfort and promote overall well-being.

Preventative Tapping

Harness the preventive power of regular tapping to ward off physical discomfort before it arises. Incorporate tapping into your daily routine as a proactive measure to release tension, promote relaxation, and maintain balance in both body and mind. By tapping regularly, you can strengthen your body's resilience and reduce the likelihood of experiencing discomfort or pain in the future.

Example Routine:

- **Morning:** Tap on the eyebrow, side of the eye, and collarbone points while repeating affirmations of health and relaxation.
- **Midday:** Take a short tapping break to address any emerging tension or stress.
- **Evening:** Wind down with a comprehensive tapping session focusing on the under eye, under nose, and top of the head points to release the day's accumulated stress.

By integrating these practices into your daily life, you create a proactive approach to managing physical discomfort, ensuring sustained well-being and comfort.

3.6 Morning and Evening Tapping Routines for Balanced Energy

Set the tone for your day with invigorating morning tapping routines and wind down peacefully in the evening with calming scripts designed to promote relaxation and restful sleep. Discover the power of consistency in maintaining balanced energy levels and customize your routines to suit your unique needs and lifestyle.

Energizing Morning Routine

Start your day on the right note with an energizing EFT tapping routine aimed at priming your body and mind for the day ahead. Begin by tapping on the eyebrow point, side of the eye, and under the eye while affirming your intentions for the day and visualizing success. Progress through each meridian point, focusing on boosting energy levels and cultivating a positive mindset to tackle challenges with vigor and enthusiasm.

Sample Morning Tapping Routine:

- **Eyebrow Point:** "I am energized."
- **Side of Eye:** "Ready for the day."
- **Under Eye:** "Feeling positive."
- **Under Nose:** "Focused and strong."
- **Chin Point:** "Excited for today."
- **Collarbone Point:** "Embracing opportunities."

- **Under Arm:** "Full of energy."
- **Top of Head:** "I am ready."

Relaxing Evening Routine

Transition gracefully from the busyness of the day to a state of relaxation and ease with a soothing evening tapping script. Tap on the collarbone point, under the arm, and top of the head while releasing tension, letting go of stressors, and inviting a sense of calm and tranquility into your body and mind. With each tap, prepare yourself for restful sleep and rejuvenation, allowing the day's worries to melt away.

Sample Evening Tapping Routine:

- **Eyebrow Point:** "Releasing the day."
- **Side of Eye:** "Letting go of stress."
- **Under Eye:** "Feeling calm."
- **Under Nose:** "Inviting peace."
- **Chin Point:** "Relaxing deeply."
- **Collarbone Point:** "Ready for rest."
- **Under Arm:** "Embracing tranquility."
- **Top of Head:** "I am at peace."

Customizing Your Routine

Tailor your morning and evening tapping routines to align with your individual needs and preferences. Experiment with different tapping scripts, affirmations, and visualizations to create a routine that resonates with you and supports your overall well-being. Whether you prefer a shorter, more focused routine or a longer, more comprehensive one, find what works best for you and make it a consistent part of your daily ritual.

Consistency for Energy Balance

Emphasize the importance of consistency in practicing morning and evening tapping routines for maintaining balanced energy levels and overall well-being. Commit to making tapping a regular part of your daily routine, setting aside dedicated time each morning and evening to tap into your inner strength, cultivate resilience, and nurture your body and mind. By prioritizing consistency, you can reap the benefits of balanced energy and vitality throughout the day and night.

These morning and evening tapping routines offer a holistic approach to promoting balanced energy levels and enhancing overall well-being. Incorporate them into your daily life with intention and commitment, and experience the transformative power of EFT in supporting your journey toward greater vitality and resilience.

Discover more detailed tapping scripts, including morning and evening routines, in the 'EFT Scripts: Transformative Tapping for Every Journey' section at the back of the book. These scripts serve as a starting point for your tapping journey, allowing you to customize and tailor your own morning and evening routines to align with your unique needs and goals.

4

Addressing Emotional Pain

4.1 Healing from Past Trauma: A Gentle Approach

In the realm of emotional healing, addressing past trauma is often a crucial step toward reclaiming one's sense of peace and wholeness. Through the gentle yet potent practice of EFT, individuals can embark on a journey of healing and transformation. This section serves as a compassionate guide, offering insights and structured tapping scripts designed to facilitate gentle trauma release.

Safety First

Creating a safe and secure environment is paramount to the healing process. By establishing a sense of safety, individuals can feel empowered to explore and process traumatic memories with greater ease and confidence. Emphasizing the importance of safety sets the stage for healing to unfold organically, free from unnecessary stress or distress.

Layer by Layer

Addressing trauma incrementally allows healing to unfold at a manage-able and sustainable pace. Rather than diving headfirst into the depths of past wounds, EFT offers a gentle and systematic approach. By peeling back the layers of pain and discomfort one step at a time, individuals can gradually unravel the knots of trauma, paving the way for profound healing and liberation.

Support Systems

While EFT provides a powerful tool for self-healing, having a profes-sional support system can offer invaluable guidance and assistance. Therapy, counseling, or support groups can provide the resources needed to navigate the complexities of trauma with greater resilience and strength. Surrounding oneself with a supportive network of individuals who understand and validate their experiences can empower individuals to confront and overcome past trauma.

Tapping Practice for Trauma:

Setup Statement: Tap on the Karate Chop point while repeating: "Even though I have this trauma, I deeply and completely accept myself."
   Tapping Script:

- Eyebrow Point (EB): "This pain."
- Side of Eye (SE): "This fear."
- Under Eye (UE): "This anxiety."
- Under Nose (UN): "This guilt."
- Chin Point (CH): "This anger."
- Collarbone (CB): "This sadness."

- Under Arm (UA): "This grief."
- Top of Head (TH): "This trauma."

Repetition: Allow yourself to feel and release the emotions with each tap. Repeat the script as needed until you notice a shift in your emotional state.

Affirmations for Healing Trauma:

- "I am safe and secure as I heal from my past."
- "I release the darkness and welcome the light."
- "It is now safe for me to release all of my childhood traumas and move into love."

Testimonial: *"Through tapping, I reconnected with my body and released the incredible fear, anxiety, and guilt I had felt for years. EFT helped me feel safe in my own body again, allowing me to move forward with confidence and peace." - Ella*

For a more detailed tapping script on healing past trauma, refer to the section titled "EFT Scripts: Transformative Tapping for Every Journey" at the back of this book.

Note: If you feel overwhelmed during this process, seek support from a therapist or counselor trained in trauma-informed care. Healing from trauma is a personal journey, and having professional guidance can provide additional safety and support.

4.2 Conquering Anxiety and Fear: Tapping Scripts for Peace

As we gently navigate the process of healing from past trauma, it's essential to also address the anxiety and fear that may linger in its wake. Anxiety and fear can dominate our lives, preventing us from experiencing peace. By harnessing the power of EFT tapping, we can develop personalized strategies to ease anxiety, release fear, and cultivate inner peace. Let's explore how tapping scripts tailored for peace can guide us through this transformative journey.

Identifying Triggers

Anxiety and fear can be triggered by various situations, thoughts, or sensations. Take some time to identify your specific triggers, such as social situations, public speaking, or health concerns. Once you've identified your triggers, you can prepare specific tapping scripts to address them effectively. Addressing these small traumas or fears through tapping can lead to significant improvements in overall anxiety levels.

Daily Tapping Routines

Incorporating tapping into your daily routine can help lower general anxiety levels over time. Consider starting your day with a calming tapping routine to set a peaceful tone for the day ahead. Similarly, ending your day with a relaxation-focused tapping session can help release any built-up tension and promote restful sleep.

Emergency Anxiety Relief

When anxiety or panic strikes, having quick-tap techniques at your disposal can provide immediate relief. Practice simple tapping scripts that you can use anytime, anywhere, to help soothe your nervous system and regain a sense of calm. Remember to breathe deeply as you tap and focus on releasing tension from your body.

Soothing Words and Phrases

Incorporating calming affirmations into your tapping practice can enhance feelings of peace and tranquility to manage anxiety and fear. Experiment with affirmations such as "I am safe and secure," "I trust in my ability to handle challenges," "I am calm and centered," "I release all tension and embrace tranquility," or "I choose peace over fear." Repeat these affirmations aloud or silently as you tap on the designated meridian points.

Tapping Script for Anxiety Relief

Setup Statement: Tap on the Karate Chop point while repeating: "Even though I feel anxious, I deeply and completely accept myself."
   Tapping Script:

- Eyebrow Point (EB): "This anxiety."
- Side of Eye (SE): "This fear."
- Under Eye (UE): "This tension."
- Under Nose (UN): "This worry."
- Chin Point (CH): "This stress."
- Collarbone (CB): "This nervousness."
- Under Arm (UA): "This unease."

· Top of Head (TH): "This anxiety."

Repetition: Allow yourself to feel and release the anxiety with each tap. Repeat the script as needed until you notice a shift in your emotional state.

For additional tapping scripts and more detailed guidance on managing anxiety and fear, refer to the section titled "EFT Scripts: Transformative Tapping for Every Journey" at the back of this book.

Note: If anxiety or fear feels overwhelming, consider seeking support from a therapist or counselor trained in EFT or other therapeutic methods. Having professional guidance can provide extra support and ensure you navigate the healing process safely and effectively.

By integrating these practices into your daily life, you can develop effective strategies to manage anxiety and fear, paving the way for a calmer, more peaceful existence. Embrace the power of tapping as a tool for emotional resilience and inner peace.

4.3 Overcoming Depression with EFT: A Path to Light

As we move forward from addressing anxiety and fear, it's essential to explore how EFT can also be a powerful tool for overcoming depression. Depression can feel like a heavy cloud, obscuring hope and joy. EFT offers a path to light by gently guiding you through the darkness, helping to alleviate symptoms, instill hope, and reconnect you with the joy in your life.

Tapping Through the Darkness

Depression often brings with it a sense of numbness, hopelessness, and overwhelming sadness. EFT can help break through these barriers by addressing the emotional and energetic imbalances that contribute to these feelings. By tapping on specific meridian points and acknowledging feelings of sadness and hopelessness, we can begin to instill hope and combat negative self-talk.

Depression often stems from unresolved emotional pain and limiting beliefs. By addressing these core emotional issues through tapping, significant shifts in depressive symptoms can occur. EFT allows us to gently process and release these underlying emotions, creating space for healing and transformation.

Tapping Script for Depression Relief

Setup Statement: Tap on the Karate Chop point while repeating: "Even though I feel depressed, I deeply and completely accept myself."
Tapping Script:

- Eyebrow Point (EB): "This sadness."
- Side of Eye (SE): "This hopelessness."
- Under Eye (UE): "This numbness."
- Under Nose (UN): "This despair."
- Chin Point (CH): "This heaviness."
- Collarbone (CB): "This darkness."
- Under Arm (UA): "This isolation."
- Top of Head (TH): "This depression."

Repetition: Allow yourself to feel and release the depression with each

56

tap. Repeat the script as needed until you notice a shift in your emotional state.

For the full depression relief tapping script and other tapping scripts for this section, refer to the section titled "EFT Scripts: Transformative Tapping for Every Journey" at the back of this book. These scripts serve as a starting point, and you are encouraged to customize them to suit your unique needs and goals.

Affirmations for Hope

Affirmations play a crucial role in combating the negative self-talk that often accompanies depression. They help reprogram the subconscious mind, planting seeds of hope and positivity. Here are some affirmations to use during your tapping sessions:

- "I am worthy of love and happiness."
- "I am open to the possibility of feeling better each day."
- "I release the darkness and welcome the light."
- "I am deserving of a joyful and fulfilling life."
- "Every day, in every way, I am getting better and better."

Creating a Supportive Routine

Consistency is key when using EFT to manage depression. Establishing a daily tapping routine can provide structure and support, helping you to maintain mental and emotional balance. Here's a suggested routine:

- **Morning**: Start your day with a tapping script focused on positive affirmations and setting intentions for the day. This helps to set a positive tone and mindset.

- **Midday**: Take a few minutes to tap on any stress or negative emotions that have arisen during the day. This can prevent the buildup of emotional distress.
- **Evening**: Use a tapping script to release any remaining stress or negative feelings from the day, promoting relaxation and restful sleep.

Connecting with Joy

Depression often robs us of our ability to feel joy and pleasure. EFT can help you reconnect with these positive emotions by clearing the energetic blockages that dampen your spirit. Begin by acknowledging the current absence of joy in your life, then invite positive emotions through tapping scripts focused on cultivating happiness and contentment.

Using EFT to Reconnect with Joy

- **Acknowledging the Absence of Joy**: Begin your tapping session by acknowledging the current absence of joy and pleasure in your life. Start by tapping on the eyebrow point, side of the eye, and under the eye while verbalizing any feelings of sadness, emptiness, or lack of joy.
- **Inviting Positive Emotions**: As you move to the collarbone point, under the arm, and top of the head, focus on inviting positive emotions into your life. Use affirmations such as, "I am open to feeling joy and pleasure again," and visualize moments that bring you happiness.
- **Creating Space for Joy**: Continue the tapping script by creating a mental and emotional space for joy. Tap through each meridian point while affirming, "I deserve to feel happy and joyful," and imagine filling that space with positive experiences and feelings.

Incorporate tapping into your daily routine to reinforce the presence of joy in your life. Use short tapping sessions in the morning to set a positive tone for your day and in the evening to reflect on joyful moments.

Use supportive affirmations during your tapping sessions to strengthen your connection to joy. Examples include:

- "I am worthy of happiness."
- "Joy is a natural part of my life."
- "I embrace moments of pleasure and happiness."

Consistency is Key

Maintaining a consistent EFT routine is crucial for reconnecting with joy. Regular tapping helps reinforce positive neural pathways and supports emotional well-being. Incorporate these exercises into your routine, and over time, you'll begin to notice shifts in your emotional state. Remember, healing from depression is a journey, and EFT can be a powerful ally in finding your path to light.

4.4 Tapping for Self-Esteem: Cultivating Love and Acceptance

Embarking on a journey of self-esteem and self-acceptance with EFT tapping opens doors to profound healing and transformation. Here, we explore actionable techniques to build a positive self-image, overcome self-doubt, affirm worth, and celebrate personal victories.

Building a Positive Self-Image

Begin by tapping into the power of EFT to construct a positive self-image. Through tailored tapping scripts, address underlying beliefs and emotions that influence self-esteem. By tapping on meridian points while focusing on affirmations of self-worth and acceptance, lay the foundation for a resilient and nurturing self-image.

Tapping Script for Positive Self-Image

Setup Statement: Tap on the Karate Chop point while repeating: "Even though I doubt my worth, I deeply and completely accept myself."
Tapping Script:

- Eyebrow Point (EB): "I feel this self-doubt."
- Side of Eye (SE): "I've believed these negative thoughts for so long."
- Under Eye (UE): "I'm ready to let go of these limiting beliefs."
- Under Nose (UN): "I choose to see myself through a lens of love and acceptance."
- Chin Point (CH): "I am worthy of self-love and respect."
- Collarbone Point (CB): "I embrace my strengths and uniqueness."
- Under Arm (UA): "I release any feelings of inadequacy."
- Top of Head (TH): "I am building a positive self-image every day."

Overcoming Self-Doubt

EFT serves as a gentle yet potent tool to challenge and overcome inner critic voices. Employ strategies such as the "Movie Technique," where we visualize ourselves succeeding and tap through any negative emotions that arise. By confronting self-doubt head-on and tapping on meridian points, disrupt the patterns of negativity and cultivate a compassionate inner dialogue.

Tapping Script for Overcoming Self-Doubt

Setup Statement: Tap on the Karate Chop point while repeating: "Even though I have this self-doubt, I accept myself and how I feel."
Tapping Script:

- Eyebrow Point (EB): "This self-doubt holds me back."
- Side of Eye (SE): "I've been afraid of failure."
- Under Eye (UE): "I'm ready to release this fear."
- Under Nose (UN): "I trust in my abilities."
- Chin Point (CH): "I believe in my potential."
- Collarbone Point (CB): "I am capable and strong."
- Under Arm (UA): "I release these doubts."
- Top of Head (TH): "I embrace my confidence."

Teaching Affirmations for Self-Worth and Capabilities

Crafting affirmations that resonate with your heart and align with your aspirations is key to fostering self-esteem. Begin by identifying areas where you seek affirmation, such as confidence, competence, or self-love. Then, formulate positive statements that affirm these qualities.
Examples of Affirmations:

- "I am worthy of love and respect."
- "I trust in my abilities to overcome challenges."
- "I am open to the possibility of feeling better each day."
- "I am deserving of a joyful and fulfilling life."
- "Every day, in every way, I am getting better and better."

Repeat these affirmations during EFT tapping sessions, allowing them to permeate your subconscious mind and instill a deep sense of self-worth.

Celebrating Small Wins

With EFT tapping, every step towards self-esteem is cause for celebration. Use tapping to reinforce and celebrate personal achievements, no matter how small. By acknowledging progress and embracing victories, cultivate a sense of pride and accomplishment. Celebrating small wins nurtures self-esteem, fostering a positive outlook and a resilient spirit.

Tapping Script for Celebrating Small Wins

Setup Statement: Tap on the Karate Chop point while repeating: "Even though I often overlook my achievements, I deeply and completely accept myself."
Tapping Script:

- Eyebrow Point (EB): "I acknowledge my progress."
- Side of Eye (SE): "I am proud of my efforts."
- Under Eye (UE): "Every step forward is a victory."
- Under Nose (UN): "I celebrate my accomplishments."
- Chin Point (CH): "I am proud of myself."
- Collarbone Point (CB): "I embrace my successes."
- Under Arm (UA): "I celebrate my journey."
- Top of Head (TH): "I am proud of who I am becoming."

For detailed scripts on building a positive self-image tapping script, refer to the section titled "EFT Scripts: Transformative Tapping for Every Journey" at the back of the book. These scripts serve as invaluable companions on your journey towards cultivating love, acceptance, and unwavering self-esteem.

By integrating these practices into your daily routine, you can gradually reshape your self-perception, build confidence, and cultivate a deep sense of self-worth. Remember, the journey to self-esteem and self-acceptance is ongoing, and every step you take is a step toward greater love and appreciation for yourself.

4.5 Managing Anger and Forgiveness: EFT for Emotional Balance

Anger and the inability to forgive can weigh heavily on our emotional and physical well-being. Navigating the tumultuous landscape of these emotions with EFT Tapping provides a path to emotional equilibrium and inner peace. This section equips readers with transformative tapping scripts to dissolve anger, foster forgiveness, and restore emotional balance.

Tapping Away Anger

Anger can manifest in various ways, from mild irritation to intense rage. EFT can help by addressing the underlying emotions and beliefs that fuel anger. Harness the healing power of EFT tapping to release pent-up anger and resentment. Through targeted tapping scripts, we navigate through layers of intense emotion, tapping on meridian points while acknowledging and validating feelings of anger. With each tap, we invite a sense of calm and tranquility to replace turbulent emotions, fostering inner peace and emotional clarity.

Tapping Script for Releasing Anger

Setup Statement: Tap on the Karate Chop point while repeating: "Even though I have all this anger, I deeply and completely love and accept myself."

- Karate Chop Point: "Even though it's so hard to let go of this anger, I choose to release it now."
- Karate Chop Point: "Even though I feel justified in my anger, I am open to finding peace."

Reminder Phrases:

- Eyebrow: "This anger..."
- Side of Eye: "Towards this person..."
- Under Eye: "Or this situation..."
- Under Nose: "It's so hard to let it go..."
- Under Mouth: "Because I feel I was right..."
- Collarbone: "And I don't want to forgive them..."
- Under Arm: "But it's time to release this anger..."
- Top of Head: "Letting go, even just a little bit..."

Closing Statement: Take a deep breath and notice how you feel.

Forgiveness Scripts

Forgiveness is a transformative practice that can shift our entire outlook on life. As the quote eloquently puts it, "Forgiveness is the fragrance that the violet sheds on the heel that has crushed it." By forgiving others and ourselves, we release the burden of anger and open our hearts to love and compassion. Forgiveness is not about condoning harmful behavior but rather freeing yourself from the emotional burden. It allows you to move forward without being tethered to past hurts.

Facilitate the profound process of forgiveness, both towards oneself and others, with specialized tapping scripts. By tapping through feelings of hurt, betrayal, and resentment, we create space for forgiveness to flourish. Through compassionate tapping, we soften the barriers to forgiveness, allowing healing and reconciliation to take root.

Self-Forgiveness Script

Setup Statement: Tap on the Karate Chop point while repeating: "Even though I struggle to forgive myself for [specific issue], I deeply and completely accept myself."
   Tapping Script:

- Eyebrow (EB): "Struggling to forgive myself."
- Side of Eye (SE): "This guilt and regret..."
- Under Eye (UE): "It's hard to let go..."
- Under Nose (UN): "I made mistakes..."
- Under Mouth (UM): "But I am human..."
- Collarbone (CB): "I choose to forgive myself..."
- Under Arm (UA): "And find peace within..."
- Top of Head (TH): "I am worthy of forgiveness."

Forgiving Others Script

Setup Statement: Tap on the Karate Chop point while repeating: "Even though I feel resentment towards [person/event], I choose to release this resentment and find peace within myself."
   Tapping Script:

- Eyebrow (EB): "Resentment towards [person/event]..."
- Side of Eye (SE): "This hurt and betrayal..."
- Under Eye (UE): "It's hard to let go..."
- Under Nose (UN): "I feel so wronged..."
- Under Mouth (UM): "But holding on hurts me..."
- Collarbone (CB): "I choose to release this resentment..."
- Under Arm (UA): "And embrace forgiveness..."
- Top of Head (TH): "I am open to peace."

Closing Statement: Take a deep breath and notice how you feel.

Understanding the Root of Anger

Delve into the deeper layers of emotion to uncover the root causes of anger. Explore past traumas, unresolved conflicts, and unmet needs that fuel anger. By shining a light on the underlying emotions, we pave the way for healing and transformation, freeing ourselves from the chains of anger and resentment.

Restoring Emotional Equilibrium

EFT offers invaluable techniques for restoring emotional balance in the aftermath of anger. Utilize grounding exercises, deep breathing, and tapping on calming points to soothe frazzled nerves and regain composure. With each tap, we reclaim our inner peace and serenity, emerging from moments of anger with renewed clarity and resilience.

Calming Script for Restoring Emotional Equilibrium

Setup Statement: Tap on the Karate Chop point while repeating: "Even though I feel frazzled and overwhelmed, I deeply and completely love and accept myself."

Tapping Script:

- Eyebrow (EB): "This stress..."
- Side of Eye (SE): "This tension..."
- Under Eye (UE): "I feel it in my body..."
- Under Nose (UN): "It's overwhelming..."
- Under Mouth (UM): "I choose to release this stress..."
- Collarbone (CB): "Finding calm within..."
- Under Arm (UA): "Reclaiming my peace..."
- Top of Head (TH): "I am calm and centered..."

Closing Statement: Take a deep breath and notice how you feel.

Affirmations for Anger and Forgiveness

Incorporating affirmations into your EFT practice can enhance the healing process. Use these affirmations to support your journey towards emotional balance:

- "I am at peace with my emotions."
- "I release anger and embrace calm."
- "Forgiveness sets me free."
- "I choose peace over resentment."
- "I am open to healing and transformation."
- "I am worthy of forgiveness and compassion."
- "I forgive myself and others, releasing the past."

For detailed scripts, refer to the section titled "EFT Scripts: Transformative Tapping for Every Journey" at the back of the book. These scripts serve as guiding lights on the path to emotional balance and forgiveness, empowering readers to navigate the complexities of anger and forgiveness with grace and compassion.

5

Transforming Physical Health

5.1 EFT for Chronic Pain Management: A New Hope

Understanding Pain Signals

Learning to interpret pain signals is the first step in effectively managing chronic pain with EFT tapping. Pain signals can vary widely, from sharp and stabbing to dull and throbbing sensations. By tuning into these signals, individuals can gain valuable insights into the nature of their pain and identify specific areas for EFT intervention. For instance, pinpointing whether the pain is localized or radiating, constant or intermittent, can help tailor tapping techniques accordingly. Through mindful observation and awareness, individuals can harness the power of EFT tapping to address their pain at its source, promoting relief and healing.

Mind-Body Connection

The mind-body connection plays a crucial role in chronic pain management, and the relationship between emotional well-being and physical pain is intricate. Emotional stress and trauma can exacerbate physical pain, creating a vicious cycle of discomfort. EFT tapping offers a unique approach by addressing both the emotional and physical components of pain, restoring balance and harmony to the body-mind system.

Pain Diary

Keeping a pain diary can be a valuable tool in chronic pain management. By tracking pain levels, triggers, and tapping sessions, individuals can gain insights into their condition and refine their tapping techniques accordingly. This proactive approach empowers individuals to take control of their pain and track their progress towards healing.

Tapping Script for Chronic Pain Relief

Setup Statement: Karate Chop Point: "Even though I have this chronic pain, I deeply and completely accept myself."
  Tapping Script:

- Eyebrow Point (EB): "This pain."
- Side of Eye (SE): "This discomfort."
- Under Eye (UE): "This tension."
- Under Nose (UN): "This stress."
- Chin Point (CH): "This frustration."
- Collarbone (CB): "This heaviness."
- Under Arm (UA): "This tightness."
- Top of Head (TH): "This chronic pain."

Repetition: Allow yourself to feel and release the pain with each tap. Repeat the script as needed until you notice a shift in your emotional and physical state.

Testimonials

Real-life testimonials provide tangible evidence of the effectiveness of EFT tapping in managing chronic pain. Here are some testimonies based on real experiences:

Adrian's Journey to Relief: Adrian had been suffering from debilitating pain for four years. After reading about EFT in a book she found at a local bookstore, she decided to give it a try. To her surprise, after just two sessions, her pain significantly diminished. Now, nearly two years later, Adrian is pain-free and has returned to doing the activities she loves. "I had tried everything else with no relief. Whatever the tapping does, it worked," she says.

Mary's Migraines: Mary, a 45-year-old woman, had been battling chronic migraines for over a decade. Despite trying various treatments, her migraines persisted, affecting her ability to work and enjoy life. After discovering EFT tapping, Mary was initially skeptical but decided to give it a try. She began incorporating tapping sessions into her daily routine, focusing on releasing stress and tension stored in her body. Within a few weeks, Mary noticed a significant reduction in the frequency and intensity of her migraines. Today, Mary continues to use EFT tapping as part of her self-care routine and experiences fewer migraines, allowing her to live a more fulfilling life.

John's Knee Pain: John, a 55-year-old man, had been suffering from chronic knee pain due to osteoarthritis. Despite undergoing multiple surgeries and trying various pain medications, he still experienced discomfort on a daily basis. Feeling frustrated and hopeless, John decided to explore alternative therapies and discovered EFT tapping. With guidance from a certified EFT practitioner, John learned specific tapping scripts tailored to address his knee pain. As he continued to tap regularly, John noticed a gradual decrease in his pain levels and an increase in mobility. Over time, he experienced significant improvement in his knee function, allowing him to engage in activities he had previously avoided. John's success story serves as a testament to the transformative potential of EFT tapping in managing chronic pain and reclaiming one's quality of life.

These testimonials and case studies emphasize the transformative power of EFT tapping in providing relief from chronic pain and restoring hope for those who suffer.

Additional Research

Research supports the effectiveness of EFT tapping in managing chronic pain. A study conducted by Dr. Peta Stapleton in 2016 revealed significant improvements in pain severity, impact of pain, and mental health following EFT sessions. Participants reported a 12% reduction in pain severity, an 18% decrease in the impact of pain, a 30% decrease in depression, a 42% decrease in anxiety, and a 38% decrease in stress after just one tapping session.

5.2 Tapping for Weight Loss: Addressing Emotional Eating

Understanding Emotional Triggers

Emotional eating often stems from underlying emotional triggers such as stress, boredom, or anxiety. In this section, we will explore the process of identifying these triggers and developing targeted tapping solutions to address them. By gaining awareness of our emotional patterns and the specific situations that trigger overeating, we can begin to break free from the cycle of emotional eating and find healthier ways to cope with our emotions.

Identifying Emotional Triggers

Let's embark on a journey of self-discovery to uncover the emotional triggers behind your eating habits. Take a moment to reflect on the situations or emotions that often lead to overeating. Is it stress from work or relationships? Boredom? Anxiety? By recognizing these triggers, you're taking the first step towards regaining control over your eating patterns.

Developing Targeted Tapping Solutions

Now that you've identified your emotional triggers, let's create personalized tapping solutions to address them. Grab a pen and paper, and jot down the emotions and thoughts that arise when you experience these triggers. Then, with tapping in mind, consider how you can reframe these thoughts and emotions to cultivate a healthier relationship with food. Together, we'll craft tapping scripts tailored to your specific triggers, helping you navigate through them with grace and resilience.

Tapping Script for Emotional Eating

Setup Statement: Tap on the Karate Chop point while repeating: "Even though I feel the urge to eat when I'm stressed, I deeply and completely accept myself."

  Tapping Script:

- **Eyebrow Point (EB):** "This urge to eat."
- **Side of Eye (SE):** "This stress."
- **Under Eye (UE):** "This boredom."
- **Under Nose (UN):** "This anxiety."
- **Chin Point (CH):** "These cravings."
- **Collarbone (CB):** "This emotional eating."
- **Under Arm (UA):** "This feeling of needing comfort."
- **Top of Head (TH):** "I choose to find healthier ways to cope."

Repetition: Allow yourself to feel and release the emotions with each tap. Repeat the script as needed until you notice a shift in your emotional state.

Cultivating Healthy Habits

Tapping can be a powerful tool for reinforcing positive behaviors and cultivating healthy habits. Whether it's making mindful food choices or staying consistent with exercise, tapping scripts can support and encourage lasting changes, empowering you to embrace a healthier lifestyle.

Promoting Body Positivity

Negative body image and self-esteem issues often contribute to disordered eating patterns. In this section, we will introduce tapping exercises aimed at promoting body positivity and self-acceptance. By tapping on specific meridian points while affirming self-love and acceptance, readers can begin to shift their perspective and cultivate a more positive relationship with their bodies.

Tapping Script for Body Positivity

Setup Statement: Tap on the Karate Chop point while repeating: "Even though I struggle with my body image, I deeply and completely accept myself."

Tapping Script:

- **Eyebrow Point (EB):** "This negative body image."
- **Side of Eye (SE):** "These feelings of inadequacy."
- **Under Eye (UE):** "This self-criticism."
- **Under Nose (UN):** "This lack of self-love."
- **Chin Point (CH):** "These harsh judgments."
- **Collarbone (CB):** "I choose to love and accept myself."
- **Under Arm (UA):** "I embrace my body as it is."
- **Top of Head (TH):** "I am worthy of self-love."

Repetition: Allow yourself to feel and release the negative body image with each tap. Repeat the script as needed until you notice a shift towards self-acceptance.

Sustaining Motivation

Maintaining motivation and commitment to a healthy lifestyle can be challenging, especially when faced with setbacks or obstacles. In this final section, we will discuss strategies for sustaining motivation with EFT. From setting realistic goals to practicing self-compassion, readers will learn how tapping can help them stay focused and resilient on their weight loss journey.

Tapping Script for Sustaining Motivation

Setup Statement: Tap on the Karate Chop point while repeating: "Even though I struggle to stay motivated, I deeply and completely accept myself."
  Tapping Script:

- **Eyebrow Point (EB):** "This lack of motivation."
- **Side of Eye (SE):** "These setbacks."
- **Under Eye (UE):** "This feeling of giving up."
- **Under Nose (UN):** "This frustration."
- **Chin Point (CH):** "These obstacles."
- **Collarbone (CB):** "I can stay motivated."
- **Under Arm (UA):** "I am resilient."
- **Top of Head (TH):** "I am committed to my health."

Repetition: Allow yourself to feel and release the lack of motivation with each tap. Repeat the script as needed until you feel more inspired and focused.

Research Insights

Research has shown that EFT tapping can be highly effective for weight loss by addressing emotional eating and reducing stress, which are significant contributors to weight gain. Studies have demonstrated that EFT can reduce food cravings, improve emotional eating patterns, and support long-term weight management. For instance, a 2018 study found that participants who engaged in EFT lost an average of one pound per week and continued to lose weight over the following year. Another study in 2019 revealed a 74% reduction in craving levels after a four-day EFT workshop.

Moreover, EFT has been shown to lower cortisol levels, the stress hormone linked to weight gain, by 43%. This reduction in cortisol not only helps in weight management but also improves overall mental health by decreasing anxiety and depression levels.

Testimonials

To provide tangible evidence of EFT's effectiveness in managing weight loss and addressing emotional eating, we include real-life testimonials. These stories showcase individuals who have successfully used EFT to overcome emotional eating, cultivate healthy habits, and transform their relationship with food and their bodies.

Thomas's Success *Thomas had a history of yo-yo dieting and negative self-image. After incorporating EFT into his daily routine, focusing on body positivity and healthy habits, he experienced a significant shift. "EFT helped me understand my emotional triggers and gave me the tools to deal with them constructively. I'm not only losing weight, but I'm also gaining confidence and self-acceptance."*

Emily's Transformation *Emily had battled with weight issues since her* *teenage years, often turning to food for comfort during times of emotional distress. After learning about EFT, she began using it to address her feelings of anxiety and sadness. Emily tapped on specific points while acknowledging her emotions and gradually noticed a decrease in her emotional eating. Within a year, Emily had lost 30 pounds and felt more in control of her life. She says, "EFT gave me a sense of empowerment. It was like a switch turned on, and I started to choose healthier ways to cope with my emotions."*

David's Path to Health *David was skeptical about EFT at first but decided to give it a try after struggling with his weight for many years. He used tapping to deal with his late-night cravings and feelings of guilt associated with overeating. By addressing these deep-seated emotions, David found it easier to stick to his diet and exercise routine. In eight months, David lost 40 pounds and felt more energetic than ever. He shared, "EFT helped me break the cycle of emotional eating. It's not just about the weight loss, but about feeling better mentally and physically."*

By integrating these real-life experiences, you can see the potential of EFT to bring about meaningful change in your own weight loss journeys. For detailed tapping scripts designed to support your weight loss journey, please refer to the "EFT Scripts: Transformative Tapping for Every Journey" section at the back of this book.

5.3 EFT for Insomnia: Scripts for a Restful Sleep

A good night's sleep is essential for overall health and well-being, yet many struggle with insomnia and restless nights. Insomnia can significantly impact your quality of life, affecting both physical and mental health. EFT tapping provides an effective, natural way to address the underlying causes of insomnia and promote better sleep.

EFT tapping offers effective solutions to calm the mind, address sleep anxieties, and promote restful sleep. In this section, we'll explore how EFT can help you prepare for sleep, manage middle-of-the-night wakefulness, and alleviate sleep-related anxiety. We'll also discuss the importance of creating a sleep-friendly environment to support your efforts.

Preparing for Sleep

Creating a calming bedtime routine is crucial for preparing your mind and body for rest. EFT can be an integral part of this routine, helping to quiet the mind and release the stresses of the day.

Steps for Preparing for Sleep:

- **Create a Calm Environment:** Dim the lights and ensure your sleeping area is comfortable and free from distractions.
- **Bedtime Ritual:** Establish a consistent bedtime routine, such as reading a book, listening to calming music, or taking a warm bath.

Tapping Routine:

Setup Statement: Karate Chop Point: "Even though I feel restless and anxious about sleeping, I deeply and completely accept myself."

Tapping Script:

- **Eyebrow Point (EB):** "This restlessness and anxiety."
- **Side of Eye (SE):** "I choose to release this restlessness."
- **Under Eye (UE):** "Calming my mind for sleep."
- **Under Nose (UN):** "Letting go of today's stress."
- **Chin Point (CH):** "Inviting relaxation into my body."
- **Collarbone (CB):** "I release the tension in my body."
- **Under Arm (UA):** "I am ready to sleep peacefully."

- **Top of Head (TH):** "I welcome a restful night's sleep."

Repetition: Repeat the script until you feel calm and ready to sleep.

Middle-of-the-Night Waking

Waking up in the middle of the night and struggling to return to sleep can be frustrating. EFT can help you address the immediate anxiety or restlessness and guide you back to a state of relaxation.

Steps for Middle-of-the-Night Waking:

- **Stay Calm:** Avoid checking the time and remind yourself that it's okay to be awake.

Tapping Routine:

Setup Statement: Karate Chop Point: "Even though I woke up and feel anxious about not sleeping, I deeply and completely accept myself."

Tapping Script:

- **Eyebrow Point (EB):** "This anxiety about being awake."
- **Side of Eye (SE):** "I choose to release this anxiety."
- **Under Eye (UE):** "Calming my mind and body."
- **Under Nose (UN):** "I am safe and relaxed."
- **Chin Point (CH):** "Allowing myself to drift back to sleep."
- **Collarbone (CB):** "Releasing any stress in my body."
- **Under Arm (UA):** "I welcome a peaceful return to sleep."
- **Top of Head (TH):** "I am calm and ready to sleep again."

Repetition: Repeat the script until you feel ready to fall back asleep.

Sleep Anxiety

Anxiety about sleep can prevent you from getting the rest you need. Addressing this anxiety with EFT can help you create a more positive and relaxed mindset around sleep.

Steps for Addressing Sleep Anxiety

- **Acknowledge Anxiety:** Recognize and validate your feelings about sleep.

Tapping Routine:

Setup Statement: Karate Chop Point: "Even though I feel anxious about not sleeping, I deeply and completely accept myself."

Tapping Script:

- **Eyebrow Point (EB):** "This anxiety about sleep."
- **Side of Eye (SE):** "I choose to release this anxiety."
- **Under Eye (UE):** "Feeling calm and relaxed."
- **Under Nose (UN):** "Trusting my body's ability to sleep."
- **Chin Point (CH):** "Letting go of sleep-related worries."
- **Collarbone (CB):** "I am safe and ready to sleep."
- **Under Arm (UA):** "I am in control of my sleep."
- **Top of Head (TH):** "I trust my body to rest well."

Repetition: Repeat the script until you feel relaxed about sleep.

Creating a Sleep-Friendly Environment

Combining EFT with environmental changes can enhance your sleep quality. A sleep-friendly environment supports your body's natural sleep rhythms and helps reduce insomnia.

Steps for Creating a Sleep-Friendly Environment:

- **Optimize Your Bedroom:** Keep the room cool, dark, and quiet. Use blackout curtains and consider a white noise machine if needed.
- **Establish a Routine:** Go to bed and wake up at the same time every day to regulate your internal clock.

Tapping Routine:

Setup Statement: Karate Chop Point: "Even though I sometimes struggle with my sleep environment, I deeply and completely accept myself."

Tapping Script:

- **Eyebrow Point (EB):** "Creating a calm and restful space."
- **Side of Eye (SE):** "I optimize my bedroom for sleep."
- **Under Eye (UE):** "Feeling comfortable and relaxed."
- **Under Nose (UN):** "My bedroom is my sanctuary."
- **Chin Point (CH):** "I establish a soothing sleep routine."
- **Collarbone (CB):** "I am in control of my sleep environment."
- **Under Arm (UA):** "My environment supports my rest."
- **Top of Head (TH):** "I welcome a peaceful night's sleep."

Repetition: Repeat the script until you feel your environment supports your sleep.

For detailed tapping scripts that address specific aspects of insomnia, please refer to the "EFT Scripts: Transformative Tapping for Every Journey" section at the back of this book. These scripts are designed to guide you through comprehensive tapping scripts to help you achieve better sleep and improve your overall well-being.

5.4 Overcoming Fatigue: Energy-Boosting Tapping Techniques

Fatigue can stem from a variety of sources, both emotional and physical. In this section, we will explore how EFT can be used to boost energy levels, address underlying causes of fatigue, and help readers find a balance between activity and rest.

Identifying Causes of Fatigue

Fatigue is often a complex issue with multiple contributing factors. By identifying potential emotional or physical causes, readers can better tailor their tapping routines to address their specific needs.

Exploring Emotional Causes

Take a moment to reflect on any emotional factors that might be contributing to your fatigue. Are you experiencing stress, anxiety, or unresolved emotional issues? Journaling about your feelings and identifying patterns can help uncover these emotional roots.

Physical Contributors

Consider any physical aspects that might be draining your energy. This could include poor sleep, lack of exercise, or dietary habits. Keeping a log of your daily activities and energy levels can provide insights into physical causes of fatigue.

Tapping for Vitality

EFT can be a powerful tool for increasing energy levels and reducing feelings of fatigue. Below, we introduce tapping scripts designed to boost vitality and rejuvenate your body and mind.

Morning Energy Boost Script

Setup Statement: Karate Chop Point: "Even though I feel tired and sluggish, I deeply and completely accept myself."
   Tapping Script:

- **Eyebrow Point (EB):** "I feel this tiredness in my body."
- **Side of Eye (SE):** "It's hard to get started in the morning."
- **Under Eye (UE):** "I feel this lack of energy."
- **Under Nose (UN):** "I want to feel more energized."
- **Chin Point (CH):** "I choose to release this fatigue."
- **Collarbone (CB):** "I welcome vitality into my body."
- **Under Arm (UA):** "Feeling energized and refreshed."
- **Top of Head (TH):** "I am open to feeling more awake and alert."

Repetition: Repeat the script until you feel a boost in your energy levels.

Midday Rejuvenation Script

Setup Statement: Karate Chop Point: "Even though I feel a slump in my energy, I deeply and completely accept myself."
   Tapping Script:

- **Eyebrow Point (EB):** "This midday fatigue is overwhelming."
- **Side of Eye (SE):** "I feel drained and tired."

- **Under Eye (UE):** "I want to rejuvenate my energy."
- **Under Nose (UN):** "I choose to release this tiredness."
- **Chin Point (CH):** "I am revitalized and energized."
- **Collarbone (CB):** "I feel my energy returning."
- **Under Arm (UA):** "Releasing all fatigue."
- **Top of Head (TH):** "Feeling awake and full of energy."

Repetition: Repeat the script until you feel rejuvenated.

Balancing Activity and Rest

Finding the right balance between activity and rest is crucial for maintaining energy levels. EFT can help you listen to your body and mind, promoting a harmonious balance.

Daily Balance Strategy:

- **Activity Awareness:** Pay attention to how different activities affect your energy. Use tapping to reinforce positive behaviors and adjust those that drain you.
- **Rest and Recovery:** Use tapping to encourage restful practices. "Even though I feel guilty for resting, I deeply and completely accept myself." This affirmation helps in accepting the need for rest without guilt.

Incorporating Mindfulness and Rest

Combining EFT with mindfulness practices can enhance rest and recuperation. Mindfulness allows you to stay present and aware, which can amplify the benefits of tapping.

Mindfulness and EFT Routine:

85

- **Mindful Breathing:** Start with a few minutes of deep, mindful breathing to center yourself.
- **Tapping for Relaxation:** Use a simple tapping script focused on relaxation: "Even though I feel stressed, I deeply and completely accept myself."
- **Gratitude Practice:** End with a moment of gratitude, tapping on how this practice is helping you feel more balanced and rested.

By integrating these practices, you can create a powerful routine that not only boosts your energy but also fosters overall well-being.

For detailed tapping scripts designed to support your journey toward overcoming fatigue, please refer to the "EFT Scripts: Transformative Tapping for Every Journey" section at the back of this book.

6

Cultivating Abundance and Success

6.1 Tapping into Abundance: Clearing Financial Blockages

In the realm of abundance, our beliefs about money often shape our reality. Let's embark on a journey to uncover how EFT can serve as a potent tool for clearing financial blockages and welcoming abundance into our lives.

Financial Beliefs and Blockages

Take a moment to reflect on your beliefs surrounding money and abundance. Are there any limiting beliefs that may be holding you back from financial success? By identifying and acknowledging these beliefs, you're taking the first step towards transformation. Together, let's explore techniques to challenge and release these limiting beliefs, paving the way for a mindset of prosperity.

Exploring Limiting Beliefs

Begin by reflecting on your beliefs surrounding money and abundance. Are there any recurring thoughts or beliefs that may be holding you back from financial success? These limiting beliefs can manifest in various forms, such as:

- "I'm not good with money."
- "I'll never be wealthy."
- "Money is scarce, and I'll never have enough."

Challenging Limiting Beliefs

Once you've identified your limiting beliefs, it's time to challenge them. Start by questioning the validity of these beliefs. Ask yourself:

- "Is this belief based on facts or assumptions?"
- "Have I always believed this, or did it develop over time?"
- "What evidence exists to support or refute this belief?"

By critically examining your beliefs, you can begin to weaken their hold on your mindset and open yourself up to new possibilities.

Releasing Limiting Beliefs with EFT

Now, let's leverage the power of EFT to release these limiting beliefs. Create a tapping script tailored to challenge and release each specific belief. For example:

Setup Statement: Karate Chop Point: "Even though I've always believed that money is scarce, I deeply and completely accept myself and choose to release this limiting belief."

Tapping Script:

- **Eyebrow Point (EB):** "I release the belief that money is scarce."
- **Side of Eye (SE):** "I am worthy of financial abundance."
- **Under Eye (UE):** "I choose to believe in my ability to attract wealth."
- **Under Nose (UN):** "I let go of any fears about money."
- **Chin Point (CH):** "I open myself to financial opportunities."
- **Collarbone Point (CB):** "I am deserving of success and prosperity."
- **Under Arm (UA):** "I release all doubts about my financial future."
- **Top of Head (TH):** "I welcome abundance into my life."

Repetition: Repeat the script until you feel a shift in your mindset.

Affirming a Mindset of Prosperity

Finally, replace your limiting beliefs with affirmations that affirm a mindset of prosperity. Repeat these affirmations daily to reinforce your new beliefs. For example:

- "I am open to receiving abundance in all areas of my life."
- "Money flows to me easily and effortlessly."
- "I am worthy of financial success and prosperity."

Through this process of exploration, challenge, and affirmation, you'll pave the way for a mindset of prosperity, allowing abundance to flow freely into your life.

Addressing Financial Stress

Stress significantly impacts financial decision-making and overall well-being. EFT can help reduce stress, enabling you to think more clearly and make better financial decisions.

Setup Statement: Karate Chop Point: "Even though I feel stressed about my finances, I deeply and completely accept myself."

Tapping Script:

- **Eyebrow Point (EB):** "This financial stress."
- **Side of Eye (SE):** "Feeling overwhelmed by money worries."
- **Under Eye (UE):** "I choose to release this stress."
- **Under Nose (UN):** "Letting go of financial anxiety."
- **Chin Point (CH):** "Embracing calm and clarity."
- **Collarbone (CB):** "I trust in my ability to manage my finances."
- **Under Arm (UA):** "Releasing the hold of stress on my finances."
- **Top of Head (TH):** "I am calm and in control."

Repetition: Use this tapping script whenever you feel financial stress arising.

Visualization and Gratitude Practices

Visualization can be a powerful ally in manifesting abundance. By vividly imagining the life you desire, you set the stage for its manifestation. Here are some visualization techniques to integrate into your EFT practice:

- **Vision Board Creation:** Design a vision board filled with images and words that represent your financial goals and aspirations. Spend time each day tapping while visualizing yourself living the abundant life depicted on your board. Allow yourself to feel the emotions of already having achieved these goals.

- **Future Self Visualization:** Close your eyes and imagine your future self living the life of abundance you desire. Visualize yourself in detail—where you live, how you spend your days, the people you interact with, and the experiences you enjoy. Feel the joy, fulfillment, and freedom of living in alignment with your financial dreams.

- **Scripting Your Ideal Reality:** Write a detailed script describing your ideal financial situation as if it has already manifested. Include specific details about your income, savings, investments, and lifestyle. Read this script aloud while tapping, allowing the words to sink deeply into your subconscious mind and reinforce your vision of abundance.

- **Gratitude Visualization and Practices:** Gratitude is a fundamental key to unlocking abundance. Visualize yourself expressing gratitude for the abundance already present in your life. Imagine each tap amplifying the feelings of gratitude and attracting even more abundance into your experience. Focus on the abundance surrounding you—whether it's the love of family and friends, opportunities for growth, or the simple joys of everyday life.

By incorporating these visualization techniques into your EFT practice, infusing each tap with a sense of thankfulness and abundance you create a clear path to prosperity and draw abundance closer with each tap. As you shift your focus from scarcity to abundance, you'll open the floodgates to even greater prosperity.

Scientific Backing for EFT and Financial Abundance

EFT has been scientifically proven to reduce stress, which can significantly impact your financial well-being. When you're less stressed, you're able to think more clearly, make better decisions, and take proactive steps toward financial success.

A study by Dr. Dawson Church and Dr. David Feinstein measured cortisol levels before and after an hour of EFT tapping. The results showed a significant decrease in cortisol levels, indicating reduced stress. Lower stress levels can help you break free from financial blockages and create a mindset open to abundance.

For detailed tapping scripts designed to support your journey toward financial abundance, please refer to the "EFT Scripts: Transformative Tapping for Every Journey" section at the back of this book.

6.2 Enhancing Relationships through EFT: Tapping for Love and Connection

Relationship Challenges

Relationships are integral to our lives, yet they can often be a source of stress and conflict. Whether it's communication issues, unresolved arguments, or differing expectations, EFT can help address these common challenges and pave the way for healthier, more fulfilling connections.

Identifying Relationship Challenges

Reflect on current or past relationships that have been challenging. What specific issues or patterns have caused tension? Write down these challenges as they come to mind.

Tapping Routine:

Setup Statement: Karate Chop Point: "Even though I struggle with [specific relationship challenge], I deeply and completely accept myself." Karate Chop Point: "Even though I feel [emotion] when dealing with [relationship issue], I choose to find peace and understanding." Karate Chop Point: "Even though [relationship challenge] causes me stress, I am open to finding solutions and healing."

Tapping Script:

- **Eyebrow Point (EB):** "Struggling with [specific relationship challenge]."
- **Side of Eye (SE):** "Feeling [emotion] about this issue."
- **Under Eye (UE):** "This tension in my relationship."
- **Under Nose (UN):** "Worrying about [relationship challenge]."
- **Chin Point (CH):** "Feeling stressed and upset."
- **Collarbone (CB):** "This ongoing conflict."
- **Under Arm (UA):** "I want to resolve this peacefully."
- **Top of Head (TH):** "I choose to find understanding and harmony."

Repetition: Repeat this script until you feel a shift in your emotional state.

Tapping for Empathy and Understanding

Empathy and understanding are crucial for building strong, supportive relationships. Before engaging in a conversation with a partner or friend, take a few moments to focus on cultivating empathy and understanding.

Enhancing Empathy and Understanding

Before engaging in a conversation with a partner or friend, take a few moments to focus on cultivating empathy and understanding.

Setup Statement: Karate Chop Point: "Even though I sometimes struggle to understand others, I deeply and completely accept myself." Karate Chop Point: "Even though I find it hard to empathize, I choose to open my heart." Karate Chop Point: "Even though I get frustrated, I am open to understanding and connection."

Tapping Script:

- **Eyebrow Point (EB):** "Struggling to understand others."
- **Side of Eye (SE):** "Finding it hard to empathize."
- **Under Eye (UE):** "Feeling frustrated and disconnected."
- **Under Nose (UN):** "Wishing for better understanding."
- **Chin Point (CH):** "Feeling distant from others."
- **Collarbone (CB):** "This difficulty in connecting."
- **Under Arm (UA):** "I want to feel empathy and understanding."
- **Top of Head (TH):** "I choose to open my heart to others."

Positive Affirmation Script:

- **Eyebrow Point (EB):** "I am open to understanding others."
- **Side of Eye (SE):** "I cultivate empathy and compassion."

94

- **Under Eye (UE):** "I listen with an open heart."
- **Under Nose (UN):** "I am patient and understanding."
- **Chin Point (CH):** "I connect deeply with those around me."
- **Collarbone (CB):** "I foster empathy in my relationships."
- **Under Arm (UA):** "I embrace connection and understanding."
- **Top of Head (TH):** "I am a source of love and empathy."

Repetition: Repeat this script daily to enhance empathy and understanding in your relationships.

Releasing Past Relationship Trauma

Past relationship traumas can linger and impact our current connections. EFT can help you heal these wounds and open up to new, healthier relationships.

Reflecting on Past Traumas

Take some time to reflect on past relationships that have caused you pain. What specific events or patterns have left a lasting impact? Write these down to bring them to the surface.

Setup Statement: Karate Chop Point: "Even though I have pain from past relationships, I deeply and completely accept myself." Karate Chop Point: "Even though these past wounds still hurt, I choose to heal and move forward." Karate Chop Point: "Even though I fear opening up again, I am ready to release this pain."

Tapping Script:

- **Eyebrow Point (EB):** "Pain from past relationships."
- **Side of Eye (SE):** "These old wounds still hurt."
- **Under Eye (UE):** "Fear of opening up again."

- **Under Nose (UN):** "Feeling stuck in past pain."
- **Chin Point (CH):** "Worrying about being hurt again."
- **Collarbone (CB):** "This lingering relationship trauma."
- **Under Arm (UA):** "I want to release this pain."
- **Top of Head (TH):** "I choose to heal and move forward."

Positive Affirmation Script:

- **Eyebrow Point (EB):** "I am healing from past pain."
- **Side of Eye (SE):** "I release old relationship wounds."
- **Under Eye (UE):** "I am open to new, healthy connections."
- **Under Nose (UN):** "I trust in my ability to love again."
- **Chin Point (CH):** "I embrace healing and growth."
- **Collarbone (CB):** "I let go of past traumas."
- **Under Arm (UA):** "I am ready for healthy relationships."
- **Top of Head (TH):** "I open my heart to love and connection."

Repetition: Use this script regularly to help heal past relationship traumas.

Affirmations for Love and Connection

Affirmations can strengthen your intentions to cultivate love and connection in your relationships. Here are some affirmations to integrate into your EFT practice:

Creating Affirmations

Reflect on the qualities you want to cultivate in your relationships. Write down affirmations that resonate with your goals for love and connection.

Setup Statement: Karate Chop Point: "Even though I sometimes struggle with love and connection, I deeply and completely accept myself."

Tapping Script:

- **Eyebrow Point (EB):** "I am worthy of love and connection."
- **Side of Eye (SE):** "I attract healthy, loving relationships."
- **Under Eye (UE):** "I am open to deep connections."
- **Under Nose (UN):** "I give and receive love freely."
- **Chin Point (CH):** "I nurture my relationships with care."
- **Collarbone (CB):** "I embrace empathy and understanding."
- **Under Arm (UA):** "I am a source of love and positivity."
- **Top of Head (TH):** "I cultivate loving and meaningful connections."

Repetition: Repeat these affirmations daily to reinforce your intentions for love and connection.

By integrating these techniques and scripts into your EFT practice, you can overcome relationship challenges, foster deeper connections, heal past traumas, and cultivate a life filled with love and meaningful relationships.

6.3 Setting and Achieving Goals with EFT: A Strategic Approach

Achieving our goals often involves overcoming various internal obstacles and maintaining a clear, determined focus. This section will guide you through using EFT to set and achieve your goals more effectively, addressing the common challenges that arise along the way.

Goal Clarity

To achieve your goals, it's essential first to have a clear understanding of what they are and why they matter to you. This clarity helps in staying motivated and focused. Here's how you can use EFT to gain this clarity:

Identify Your Goals:

- Find a quiet place to sit comfortably.
- Take a few deep breaths to center yourself.
- Write down your goals on a piece of paper.

Explore Underlying Motivations:

- Begin tapping on the Karate Chop point and say: "Even though I feel uncertain about my goals, I deeply and completely accept myself."
- Move through the tapping points (Eyebrow, Side of Eye, Under Eye, Under Nose, Chin, Collarbone, Under Arm, and Top of Head) while reflecting on why each goal is important to you.
- Tap through the script again, focusing on the feelings and motivations behind each goal.

Tapping Routine:

Setup Statement: Karate Chop Point: "Even though I feel uncertain about my goals, I deeply and completely accept myself."
Tapping Script:

- **Eyebrow Point (EB):** "This uncertainty about my goals."
- **Side of Eye (SE):** "Wondering why these goals matter."
- **Under Eye (UE):** "Feeling unclear about my motivations."
- **Under Nose (UN):** "I want to understand my goals better."
- **Chin Point (CH):** "Exploring why these goals are important."
- **Collarbone (CB):** "Connecting with my true motivations."
- **Under Arm (UA):** "Gaining clarity on my goals."
- **Top of Head (TH):** "Feeling clear and focused."

Repetition: Repeat this script until you feel a sense of clarity and motivation.

Overcoming Procrastination

Procrastination is a common barrier to achieving goals. EFT can help you address the underlying emotions and resistance that cause procrastination:

Acknowledge the Resistance:

- Tap on the Karate Chop point: "Even though I keep putting off my tasks, I deeply and completely accept myself."
- Move through the tapping points, focusing on the emotions tied to your procrastination (e.g., fear of failure, feeling overwhelmed).

Reframe the Task:

- Continue tapping through the points while stating positive affirmations: "I choose to tackle my tasks one step at a time." "I am capable and focused."

Setup Statement: Karate Chop Point: "Even though I keep putting off my tasks, I deeply and completely accept myself."
   Tapping Script:

- **Eyebrow Point (EB):** "I keep procrastinating."
- **Side of Eye (SE):** "Feeling overwhelmed by tasks."
- **Under Eye (UE):** "Afraid of failing."
- **Under Nose (UN):** "This resistance to starting."
- **Chin Point (CH):** "Feeling stuck and unmotivated."
- **Collarbone (CB):** "I choose to take it one step at a time."
- **Under Arm (UA):** "I am capable and focused."
- **Top of Head (TH):** "I can overcome procrastination."

Repetition: Use this script whenever you feel procrastination creeping in.

Tapping for Focus and Determination

Maintaining focus and determination is crucial in pursuing goals. EFT can help strengthen these qualities:
   Enhancing Focus:

- Tap on the Karate Chop point: "Even though I get easily distracted, I deeply and completely accept myself."
- Move through the tapping points while visualizing yourself working on your goals with clear focus.

Building Determination

Tap through the script while repeating affirmations like: "I am determined to achieve my goals." "I have the resilience to overcome any obstacle."

Setup Statement: Karate Chop Point: "Even though I get easily distracted, I deeply and completely accept myself."

Tapping Script:

- **Eyebrow Point (EB):** "I get easily distracted."
- **Side of Eye (SE):** "Struggling to maintain focus."
- **Under Eye (UE):** "I want to stay focused."
- **Under Nose (UN):** "Visualizing clear focus on my goals."
- **Chin Point (CH):** "I am determined to succeed."
- **Collarbone (CB):** "Building my focus and determination."
- **Under Arm (UA):** "Overcoming distractions."
- **Top of Head (TH):** "I am focused and determined."

Repetition: Use this script daily to reinforce your focus and determination.

Celebrating Progress

Recognizing and celebrating your progress is essential for maintaining motivation. Use EFT to reinforce these positive experiences:

Acknowledge Achievements:

- Tap on the Karate Chop point:
- "Even though I don't always acknowledge my progress, I deeply and completely accept myself."
- Move through the tapping points, reflecting on recent successes

and milestones you've reached.

Celebrate Progress

Continue tapping while expressing gratitude and pride in your accomplishments: "I am proud of my progress." "I celebrate every step forward."

Setup Statement: Karate Chop Point: "Even though I don't always acknowledge my progress, I deeply and completely accept myself."

Tapping Script:

- **Eyebrow Point (EB):** "I don't always see my progress."
- **Side of Eye (SE):** "Overlooking my achievements."
- **Under Eye (UE):** "I want to acknowledge my progress."
- **Under Nose (UN):** "Reflecting on my successes."
- **Chin Point (CH):** "Feeling proud of my accomplishments."
- **Collarbone (CB):** "I celebrate my progress."
- **Under Arm (UA):** "Expressing gratitude for my achievements."
- **Top of Head (TH):** "I am proud of every step forward."

Repetition: Celebrate your progress regularly to maintain motivation.

By integrating these EFT techniques and scripts into your routine, you can achieve greater clarity, overcome procrastination, enhance your focus and determination, and celebrate your progress, thereby making your goal achievement journey more effective and fulfilling.

7

Spiritual Growth and Exploration

7.1 EFT and Chakra Clearing: Aligning Your Energy Centers

Introduction to Chakras

The chakra system, originating from ancient Eastern spiritual traditions, refers to the seven main energy centers within the body. Each chakra is associated with specific physical, emotional, and spiritual aspects, and maintaining their balance is crucial for overall well-being and vitality. Chakras play a fundamental role in emotional and spiritual balance because they serve as energetic gateways within the body, influencing both our internal state and our connection to the broader universe.

Importance of Chakra Balance

- **Energetic Flow:** Chakras are like spinning wheels of energy, and when they are balanced and open, energy flows smoothly through them. This balanced flow of energy promotes emotional stability and resilience, allowing us to navigate life's challenges with greater ease.

- **Emotional Regulation:** Each chakra is associated with specific emotions and psychological functions. When a chakra is blocked or overactive, it can lead to emotional imbalances such as anxiety, depression, or anger. By maintaining chakra balance, we can support healthy emotional regulation and cultivate greater emotional intelligence.
- **Spiritual Connection:** Chakras are also linked to our spiritual development and connection to higher consciousness. When our chakras are balanced, we may experience a greater sense of inner peace, clarity, and spiritual alignment. This alignment facilitates our ability to connect with our intuition, higher self, and the divine.
- **Physical Health:** Imbalances in the chakras can manifest as physical ailments or discomfort. For example, blockages in the heart chakra may manifest as heartache or respiratory issues, while imbalances in the throat chakra could result in communication difficulties or throat-related ailments. By addressing chakra imbalances, we can support physical healing and well-being.

Overview of the Seven Chakras

Root Chakra (Muladhara)

- **Location**: Base of the spine
- **Color**: Red
- **Associated with**: Survival, security, stability, and the physical body
- **Imbalance may manifest as**: Fear, anxiety, insecurity, or feeling disconnected from the physical world

Sacral Chakra (Swadhisthana)

- **Location**: Lower abdomen, below the navel
- **Color**: Orange
- **Associated with**: Creativity, sexuality, pleasure, and emotional balance
- **Imbalance may manifest as**: Emotional instability, lack of creativity, or issues with intimacy

Solar Plexus Chakra (Manipura)

- **Location**: Upper abdomen, near the stomach
- **Color**: Yellow
- **Associated with**: Personal power, confidence, self-esteem, and willpower
- **Imbalance may manifest as**: Low self-esteem, lack of motivation, or difficulty making decisions

Heart Chakra (Anahata)

- **Location**: Center of the chest, near the heart
- **Color**: Green (sometimes pink)
- **Associated with**: Love, compassion, forgiveness, and empathy
- **Imbalance may manifest as**: Difficulty in giving or receiving love, resentment, or heartache

Throat Chakra (Vishuddha)

- **Location**: Throat
- **Color**: Blue
- **Associated with**: Communication, self-expression, authenticity,

and speaking one's truth
- **Imbalance may manifest as**: Difficulty expressing oneself, fear of judgment, or throat-related issues

Third Eye Chakra (Ajna)

- **Location**: Between the eyebrows (forehead)
- **Color**: Indigo
- **Associated with**: Intuition, insight, imagination, and inner wisdom
- **Imbalance may manifest as**: Lack of clarity, confusion, or difficulty accessing intuition

Crown Chakra (Sahasrara)

- **Location**: Top of the head
- **Color**: Violet or white
- **Associated with**: Spiritual connection, enlightenment, divine consciousness, and unity
- **Imbalance may manifest as**: Disconnection from spirituality, close-mindedness, or existential distress

Identifying Blocked Chakras

Readers can learn to recognize signs of blocked or unbalanced chakras by tuning into physical sensations, emotions, and patterns of behavior. Understanding these indicators empowers individuals to pinpoint which chakras may require attention and clearing.

Here's a guide to help identify blocked or unbalanced chakras:
Physical Sensations: Pay attention to physical sensations or discomfort in specific areas of the body. Each chakra is associated with a

particular region, so discomfort or pain in those areas may indicate an imbalance. For example, tightness or tension in the lower back could suggest issues with the root chakra, while throat soreness might indicate imbalances in the throat chakra.

Emotional Patterns: Take note of recurring emotional patterns or challenges you face. Each chakra is linked to specific emotions, so persistent negative emotions may signal an imbalance. For instance, feelings of insecurity or fear might point to issues with the root chakra, while difficulty expressing oneself could indicate a blockage in the throat chakra.

Behavioral Patterns: Reflect on your behavioral patterns and tendencies. Notice if you consistently struggle with certain aspects of your life, such as relationships, career, or self-expression. These patterns could be connected to imbalances in corresponding chakras. For example, a lack of self-confidence and assertiveness might stem from issues with the solar plexus chakra.

Intuition and Inner Guidance: Trust your intuition and inner guidance to provide insights into your chakra health. Pay attention to intuitive nudges or gut feelings about areas of your life that feel out of alignment. Your intuition may lead you to recognize which chakras require attention and healing.

Energy Sensitivity: Develop sensitivity to energy flow within your body. Practice mindfulness and meditation to tune into subtle energetic shifts and sensations. Notice areas where energy feels blocked or stagnant, as these may correspond to imbalances in specific chakras. Regularly scanning your body's energy field can help you identify areas that need rebalancing.

EFT Tapping for Chakra Clearing

Tailored EFT tapping scripts facilitate the clearing and balancing of each chakra, aiming to release stagnant energy and resolve emotional blockages.

Example Tapping Script for the Root Chakra:

Setup Statement:

Karate Chop Point: "Even though I feel insecure and disconnected from the world, I deeply and completely accept myself."

Tapping Script:

- **Eyebrow Point (EB):** "Feeling insecure and disconnected."
- **Side of Eye (SE):** "This fear in my root chakra."
- **Under Eye (UE):** "Feeling unstable."
- **Under Nose (UN):** "I want to feel secure."
- **Chin Point (CH):** "Releasing this insecurity."
- **Collarbone (CB):** "I choose to feel grounded."
- **Under Arm (UA):** "Feeling connected to the earth."
- **Top of Head (TH):** "I am safe and secure."

Repetition: Repeat this script until you feel more grounded and secure.

Maintaining Chakra Health

Daily practices utilizing EFT are shared to support the ongoing health and balance of the chakra system. These practices include simple tapping routines, mindfulness exercises, and energy-clearing techniques to promote vitality and alignment.

Mindfulness Meditation: Practice mindfulness meditation to bring awareness to each chakra individually. Visualize each chakra as a spinning wheel of energy, starting from the root chakra at the base of the spine and moving up to the crown chakra at the top of the head. Spend a few minutes focusing on each chakra, breathing deeply and allowing any tension or blockages to release.

Chakra Balancing Affirmations: Use affirmations tailored to each chakra to promote balance and alignment. For example, for the root chakra, you might affirm, "I am grounded and secure in my physical body." For the heart chakra, you could affirm, "I am open to giving and receiving love." Repeat these affirmations daily as part of your mindfulness practice.

Energy Clearing Techniques: Incorporate energy clearing techniques such as smudging with sage to remove any negative energy or blockages from your space. Simply light the sage stick and allow the smoke to waft around your body, focusing on areas where you feel tension or imbalance. Visualize the smoke clearing away any stagnant energy and leaving you feeling refreshed and revitalized.

Chakra Stones and Crystals: Use chakra stones and crystals to support chakra healing and alignment. Choose stones that correspond to each chakra, such as garnet for the root chakra, rose quartz for the heart chakra, and amethyst for the crown chakra. Place the stones on the corresponding chakra points during meditation or carry them with you throughout the day to benefit from their healing properties.

Yoga and Movement Practices: Engage in yoga poses and movement practices that target each chakra. For example, grounding poses like Mountain Pose and Tree Pose can help balance the root chakra, while heart-opening poses like Cobra Pose and Camel Pose can support the heart chakra. Incorporate these practices into your daily routine to keep your energy flowing smoothly and promote overall vitality and alignment.

By incorporating these mindfulness exercises and energy clearing techniques into your daily routine, you can promote vitality and alignment and maintain the health of your chakra system. Experiment with different practices to find what resonates best with you, and remember to listen to your body's wisdom as you work towards greater balance and harmony.

For detailed tapping scripts that address chakra clearing and balancing, please refer to the "EFT Scripts: Transformative Tapping for Every Journey" section at the back of this book.

7.2 Tapping into Intuition: EFT for Inner Guidance

Intuition, often referred to as our inner guidance or gut feeling, plays a significant role in decision-making and spiritual connection. It is the innate ability to understand or know something instinctively without the need for conscious reasoning. By tapping into our intuition, we can access profound wisdom and guidance that transcends the limitations of logic and intellect.

Removing Blocks to Intuition

Despite its importance, many individuals experience blocks to their intuition, which can hinder their ability to connect with their inner wisdom. Common blocks include fear, self-doubt, overthinking, and past traumas. Fortunately, EFT can be a powerful tool for clearing these blocks. By tapping on specific acupressure points while focusing on the blockages, EFT helps release the underlying emotional and energetic imbalances that inhibit intuition.

EFT Scripts for Enhancing Intuition

Here are specific EFT tapping scripts designed to enhance intuitive abilities:

Setup Statement: Karate Chop Point: "Even though I struggle to trust my intuition, I deeply and completely accept myself."

Tapping Points: Repeat the setup statement while tapping through the following points and using reminder phrases like "I trust my inner guidance" and "My intuition is a valuable resource."

- **Eyebrow (EB)**: "Doubt about intuition"
- **Side of Eye (SE)**: "Fear of making wrong decisions"
- **Under Eye (UE)**: "Past experiences clouding intuition"
- **Under Nose (UN)**: "I release fear and doubt"
- **Chin (CH)**: "I trust my inner wisdom"
- **Collarbone (CB)**: "My intuition guides me wisely"
- **Under Arm (UA)**: "I am open to receiving intuitive insights"
- **Top of Head (TH)**: "I trust and honor my intuition"

Repetition: Repeat this script until you feel more connected to and trusting of your intuition.

Trusting and Acting on Intuition

Once blocks to intuition are cleared, it's essential to trust and act upon intuitive insights. Strategies for doing so include practicing mindfulness, journaling intuitive experiences, and setting intentions to follow intuition in daily life. By cultivating trust and confidence in one's intuitive abilities, individuals can navigate life's challenges with greater clarity and alignment with their higher purpose.

Mindfulness Practices

Mindfulness practices help in tuning into the present moment and quieting the mind, making it easier to hear and trust intuitive insights. Here are a few techniques:

- **Mindful Breathing**: Spend a few minutes each day focusing on your breath. This helps center your mind and opens up space for intuitive thoughts to surface.
- **Body Scan**: Conduct a mental scan of your body from head to toe, noticing any areas of tension and releasing them. This can help clear physical blocks to intuition.

Journaling Intuitive Experiences

Keeping a journal of your intuitive experiences can help strengthen your trust in your intuition. Here's how:

- **Record Insights**: Write down any intuitive insights you receive, no matter how small. This helps validate your intuition and reinforces your trust in it.
- **Reflect on Patterns**: Look for patterns or recurring themes in your intuitive insights. This can provide valuable guidance and clarity on your path.

Setting Intentions to Follow Intuition

Setting clear intentions to follow your intuition can reinforce your commitment to acting on your inner guidance. Here are some tips:

- **Daily Affirmations**: Use daily affirmations to reinforce your intention to trust and follow your intuition. For example, "I trust my inner guidance and act on my intuition with confidence."

- **Visualizations**: Visualize yourself confidently acting on your intuitive insights. This helps build confidence and prepares you to follow through in real-life situations.

By integrating these practices into your daily routine, you can enhance your intuitive abilities and navigate life with greater clarity and purpose. For more detailed tapping scripts and techniques to enhance your intuition, refer to the "EFT Scripts: Transformative Tapping for Every Journey" section at the back of this book.

7.3 EFT for Manifesting Your Dreams: Aligning Desire and Action

Principles of Manifestation

Manifestation is the process of turning your desires and dreams into reality through the power of focused intention and belief. It operates on the principle that thoughts and emotions are energy, and by aligning them with our goals, we can attract what we want into our lives. The Law of Attraction, which is a fundamental aspect of manifestation, suggests that like attracts like—positive thoughts and feelings attract positive outcomes, while negative thoughts can attract undesirable results. Understanding this principle is key to harnessing the power of EFT for manifestation.

Aligning Subconscious Beliefs

For manifestation to be effective, it is crucial to align your subconscious beliefs with your conscious desires. Often, we hold limiting beliefs that contradict our goals, which can create resistance and block our ability to manifest. EFT is a powerful tool that can help clear these subconscious blockages, making way for harmonious alignment. By tapping on specific meridian points while focusing on these limiting beliefs, you can release negative emotions and reprogram your mind to support your desires.

Steps to Align Subconscious Beliefs:

1. **Identify Limiting Beliefs**: Reflect on any negative thoughts or doubts related to your goals.
2. **Create Positive Affirmations**: Transform these limiting beliefs into positive affirmations that support your desires.
3. **Tap on Limiting Beliefs**: Use EFT tapping to address and clear these negative beliefs.
4. **Reinforce Positive Beliefs**: Integrate the positive affirmations into your tapping routine to strengthen your new, supportive beliefs.

Manifestation Tapping Routines

To assist you in manifesting your dreams, here are some EFT tapping routines tailored to specific goals:

Manifesting Abundance:

- **Setup Statement for Abundance:** "Even though I sometimes feel I am not worthy of abundance, I deeply and completely accept myself."

- **Key Tapping Points:** "I release my fears around abundance," "I attract financial prosperity."

Manifesting Love:

- **Setup Statement for love:** "Even though I feel unlovable, I deeply and completely accept myself."
- **Key Tapping Points:**"I release my fears around love," "I attract a loving relationship."

For comprehensive tapping scripts that provide the tools needed to effectively use EFT to manifest goals, please refer to the "EFT Scripts: Transformative Tapping for Every Journey" section at the back of this book.

Overcoming Manifestation Blocks

Even with a clear understanding of manifestation principles and routines, you might encounter blocks that hinder your progress. Common blocks include self-doubt, fear of failure, and past negative experiences. EFT can be used to address and overcome these obstacles, allowing you to move forward with confidence.

Steps to Overcome Manifestation Blocks:

1. **Identify Blocks:** Reflect on any feelings of resistance or negativity related to your goals.
2. **Tap on Blocks:** Use EFT to tap on the emotions and beliefs associated with these blocks.
3. **Reframe Thoughts:** Transform negative thoughts into empowering affirmations.
4. **Visualize Success:** Regularly visualize your desired outcome while

tapping to reinforce positive energy.

By integrating these EFT practices into your daily routine, you can effectively align your desires with your actions, clear any resistance, and manifest your dreams with greater ease and confidence. Remember, consistency and belief in the process are key to successful manifestation.

7.4 Cultivating Gratitude with EFT: A Path to Fulfillment

Gratitude is a transformative practice that can significantly shift your energy and perception, leading to a more fulfilling and joyful life. It helps reframe your experiences, focusing on the positive aspects rather than dwelling on the negatives. When practiced consistently, gratitude can enhance emotional resilience, improve mental health, and foster a deeper sense of connection to the world around you.

EFT for Developing a Gratitude Practice

EFT can be a powerful tool to cultivate a daily gratitude practice. By tapping on specific points while focusing on feelings of gratitude, you can amplify the positive effects and integrate them more deeply into your being.

Setup Statement: Tap on the Karate Chop point and say:

- "Even though I sometimes forget to be grateful, I deeply and completely accept myself."
- "Even though I struggle to find things to be grateful for, I deeply and completely accept myself."

- "Even though I sometimes focus on the negative, I choose to appreciate the good in my life."

Tapping Script:

- **Eyebrow (EB):** "I am grateful for this moment."
- **Side of Eye (SE):** "I appreciate the small joys in my life."
- **Under Eye (UE):** "I am thankful for the love around me."
- **Under Nose (UN):** "I recognize the abundance I have."
- **Chin (CH):** "I am grateful for my health."
- **Collarbone (CB):** "I appreciate my abilities and talents."
- **Under Arm (UA):** "I am thankful for my relationships."
- **Top of Head (TH):** "I am grateful for the opportunities I have."

Repetition: Repeat the script as needed, focusing on different aspects of your life that bring you gratitude.

Overcoming Resistance to Gratitude

It's not uncommon to feel resistance or negativity when trying to cultivate a gratitude practice. These feelings can stem from past experiences, current hardships, or deeply ingrained patterns of negative thinking. EFT can help address and transform these blocks, making it easier to embrace gratitude.

EFT for Overcoming Resistance

Setup Statement: Tap on the Karate Chop point and say:

- "Even though I feel resistant to practicing gratitude, I deeply and completely accept myself."

- "Even though it's hard for me to see the good, I choose to find gratitude in small things."
- "Even though I feel negative about my circumstances, I am open to shifting my perspective."

Tapping Script:

- **Eyebrow (EB):** "I feel resistant to gratitude."
- **Side of Eye (SE):** "It's hard to see the good."
- **Under Eye (UE):** "I feel negative about my life."
- **Under Nose (UN):** "This resistance to being grateful."
- **Chin (CH):** "These negative thoughts."
- **Collarbone (CB):** "I am open to changing my perspective."
- **Under Arm (UA):** "I choose to see the good."
- **Top of Head (TH):** "I allow myself to feel grateful."

Repetition: Repeat as necessary until you feel a shift in your perspective.

Gratitude in Challenging Times

Finding gratitude during difficult periods can be particularly challenging but also incredibly rewarding. It's during these times that gratitude can offer the most profound shift in energy and outlook, helping you navigate through hardships with greater resilience and hope.

EFT for Gratitude in Challenging Times

Setup Statement: Tap on the Karate Chop point and say:

- "Even though I am going through a tough time, I choose to find moments of gratitude."

- "Even though things are difficult right now, I am open to seeing the good."
- "Even though I feel overwhelmed by challenges, I choose to appreciate the small blessings."

Tapping Script:

- **Eyebrow (EB):** "These challenging times."
- **Side of Eye (SE):** "It's hard to feel grateful."
- **Under Eye (UE):** "I feel overwhelmed."
- **Under Nose (UN):** "This sense of struggle."
- **Chin (CH):** "I choose to find gratitude."
- **Collarbone (CB):** "I appreciate the small things."
- **Under Arm (UA):** "I am grateful for moments of peace."
- **Top of Head (TH):** "I choose to see the good even now."

Repetition: Repeat the script until you feel a sense of calm and gratitude.

By integrating these EFT techniques into your daily routine, you can harness the power of gratitude to transform your life, enhance your well-being, and foster a deeper connection with yourself and the world around you.

7.5 Connecting with the Universe: EFT for Spiritual Awakening

Understanding Spiritual Awakening

Spiritual awakening is a profound and transformative process where one becomes more aware of the deeper aspects of life and the universe. It often involves a shift in consciousness, allowing an individual to experience a greater sense of connection, purpose, and inner peace. This journey can lead to heightened intuition, deeper empathy, and a more profound understanding of oneself and the world. It is a path of self-discovery and enlightenment, where old beliefs and patterns are shed, making way for a more authentic and expansive existence.

EFT and the Higher Self

The higher self is considered the most authentic, wise, and eternal aspect of our being. It is the part of us that transcends the ego and is deeply connected to the universal consciousness. EFT tapping can be a powerful tool to connect with this higher self, helping to clear the emotional and energetic blockages that obscure our inner wisdom and guidance. By releasing fears, doubts, and limiting beliefs, EFT allows us to access the clarity and insight of our higher self, facilitating spiritual growth and awakening.

Tapping Scripts for Connection

To enhance feelings of universal connection and oneness, you can use the following EFT tapping scripts. These scripts are designed to help you tap into the higher frequencies of love, peace, and unity.

Setup Statement: "Even though I feel disconnected from the universe, I deeply and completely accept myself and am open to experiencing oneness."

Reminder Phrases:

- **Eyebrow (EB):** "I release my sense of isolation."
- **Side of Eye (SE):** "I open myself to universal love."
- **Under Eye (UE):** "I am connected to all that is."
- **Under Nose (UN):** "I feel the presence of my higher self."
- **Chin (CH):** "I trust in the wisdom of the universe."
- **Collarbone (CB):** "I am one with the cosmos."
- **Under Arm (UA):** "I embrace my spiritual connection."
- **Top of Head (TH):** "I am a part of the infinite universe."

Setup Statement: "Even though I struggle to feel my higher self's guidance, I deeply and completely accept myself and trust in my spiritual journey."

Reminder Phrases:

- **Eyebrow (EB):** "I release my doubts about my intuition."
- **Side of Eye (SE):** "I am in tune with my higher self."
- **Under Eye (UE):** "I receive divine guidance clearly."
- **Under Nose (UN):** "I am open to spiritual insight."
- **Chin (CH):** "I trust my inner wisdom."
- **Collarbone (CB):** "I am aligned with universal truth."
- **Under Arm (UA):** "I embrace my spiritual journey."
- **Top of Head (TH):** "I am guided by my higher self."

Maintaining Spiritual Connection

Maintaining a strong spiritual connection in everyday life requires consistent practice and mindfulness. Here are some tips to help you use EFT to keep this connection vibrant:

1. **Daily Tapping Practice**: Set aside a few minutes each day to tap on any feelings of disconnection or doubt. Regular practice helps

keep your energy aligned with your higher self.

2. **Meditative Tapping**: Combine EFT with meditation. As you tap, focus on your breath and visualize your connection with the universe strengthening.

3. **Affirmation Integration**: Use positive affirmations while tapping to reinforce your spiritual connection. For example, "I am always connected to the divine" or "My higher self guides me with love and wisdom."

4. **Gratitude Tapping**: Tap on feelings of gratitude for your spiritual experiences and insights. Gratitude amplifies your connection to higher frequencies and universal love.

5. **Mindful Living**: Incorporate mindfulness into your daily activities. Whether it's during a walk, while eating, or even during mundane tasks, stay present and aware of your spiritual connection.

By integrating these practices into your daily routine, you can cultivate a continuous and deepening connection with the universe, supporting your ongoing spiritual awakening. This harmonious connection can guide you through life's challenges with greater ease and help you manifest your highest potential.

7.6 EFT for Meditation and Mindfulness: Deepening Your Practice

Meditation and mindfulness are powerful practices for cultivating inner peace and awareness. Integrating EFT into these practices can enhance their effectiveness by clearing mental and emotional blocks, allowing for deeper presence and connection. Here's how EFT can support your meditation and mindfulness journey:

EFT as a Precursor to Meditation

Before diving into meditation, many practitioners find it beneficial to address any distractions or emotional turbulence that may hinder their practice. EFT serves as an effective tool for this purpose, helping to clear the mind and create a conducive internal environment for meditation. By tapping on specific thoughts, emotions, or physical sensations, you can release tension and create a sense of inner calmness, making it easier to transition into a meditative state.

EFT Tapping Exercise Before Meditation

Setup Statement: Tap on the Karate Chop point and say: "Even though I feel [emotion or distraction], I deeply and completely accept myself."
  Tapping Script:

- **Eyebrow (EB):** "I release this [emotion or distraction]."
- **Side of Eye (SE):** "Letting go of tension."
- **Under Eye (UE):** "Clearing my mind for meditation."
- **Under Nose (UN):** "Finding inner calm."
- **Chin (CH):** "I am ready to meditate."
- **Collarbone (CB):** "I feel peaceful and centered."
- **Under Arm (UA):** "Releasing all distractions."
- **Top of Head (TH):** "I am calm and focused."

Enhancing Presence with EFT

Presence lies at the heart of mindfulness, requiring a deep connection to the present moment free from mental chatter and distractions. EFT can enhance the quality of presence by addressing underlying thoughts and emotions that pull you away from the now. By tapping on issues such as anxiety, stress, or restlessness, you can clear the mental clutter and cultivate a greater sense of groundedness and clarity, allowing you to fully engage with the present moment.

EFT Tapping Exercise for Presence:

Setup Statement: Tap on the Karate Chop point and say: "Even though I struggle to stay present, I deeply and completely accept myself."

Tapping Script:

- **EB:** "I release my anxiety about the future."
- **SE:** "Letting go of past regrets."
- **UE:** "I am here and now."
- **UN:** "Finding peace in the present moment."
- **CH:** "I release all distractions."
- **CB:** "I am fully present."
- **UA:** "Embracing the here and now."
- **TH:** "I am grounded and aware."

Solutions for Common Meditation Challenges

Restlessness, distraction, and frustration are common challenges that arise during meditation. Fortunately, EFT offers practical solutions for overcoming these obstacles. By tapping on the specific challenges you encounter, such as feelings of restlessness or the inability to focus, you can address them directly and create a more harmonious meditation experience. EFT helps to release the underlying causes of these challenges, allowing you to approach meditation with greater ease and tranquility.

EFT Tapping Exercise for Meditation Challenges

Setup Statement: Tap on the Karate Chop point and say: "Even though I feel restless and distracted during meditation, I deeply and completely accept myself."

Tapping Script:

- **EB:** "This restlessness in my body."
- **SE:** "Feeling distracted."
- **UE:** "Finding it hard to focus."
- **UN:** "Releasing my frustration."
- **CH:** "I choose to relax and focus."
- **CB:** "I am calm and centered."
- **UA:** "Letting go of restlessness."
- **TH:** "I am in harmony with my meditation practice."

Incorporating EFT into Daily Life for Continuous Mindfulness

Beyond formal meditation sessions, mindfulness can be integrated into your daily life through simple practices and exercises. EFT offers a versatile approach to mindfulness, allowing you to cultivate presence and awareness in any situation. By incorporating short tapping routines into your daily routine, such as before starting work or during moments of stress, you can maintain a continuous state of mindfulness and presence throughout the day. This mindful tapping practice serves as a powerful reminder to stay grounded and centered amidst the busyness of life.

EFT Tapping Exercise for Daily Mindfulness

Setup Statement: Tap on the Karate Chop point and say: "Even though I feel overwhelmed by daily tasks, I deeply and completely accept myself."

Tapping Script:

- **EB:** "This sense of overwhelm."
- **SE:** "Feeling stressed by my to-do list."
- **UE:** "I choose to stay present."
- **UN:** "I can handle one thing at a time."
- **CH:** "Staying mindful and calm."
- **CB:** "I am grounded in the present moment."
- **UA:** "Releasing the need to rush."
- **TH:** "I am centered and focused."

By using EFT as a precursor to meditation, enhancing presence during mindfulness exercises, and addressing common meditation challenges, you can deepen your meditation and mindfulness practice. These techniques provide practical tools for cultivating inner peace, clarity, and awareness, both on and off the meditation cushion.

8

Conclusion

As we come to the end of this journey through the transformative practice of EFT tapping, take a moment to reflect on the profound healing and growth you've experienced and the endless possibilities that lie ahead.

Throughout this book, you've delved deep into the foundational principles of EFT tapping and explored its diverse applications for emotional, physical, and spiritual well-being. From understanding its basics to addressing specific life challenges, you've witnessed firsthand the versatility of this technique in promoting holistic healing and transformation.

You've learned how EFT can heal past traumas, manage stress and anxiety, overcome physical ailments, and unlock spiritual growth. By incorporating tapping into your daily routines, you've discovered its effectiveness in relieving stress, managing emotional issues, and achieving personal goals.

Reflect on the key lessons from each chapter, recognizing the potential for profound personal growth and healing that EFT offers. Draw inspiration from the testimonials and stories shared throughout, illustrating the real-life impact of EFT on individuals' lives.

Now is the time to take action and start your EFT journey. Utilize the scripts and techniques provided in this book, join EFT communities for support and guidance, and embrace the journey with an open heart and mind. Your healing and transformation begin today.

Share your experiences with EFT tapping, whether through social media, community groups, or directly with others. Your stories have the power to inspire and support others on their own healing paths.

For those eager to delve deeper into EFT tapping, additional resources are available. Explore websites, courses, events, YouTube, apps, and community forums to continue your education and practice, and to connect with like-minded individuals on similar journeys.

As we conclude this book, remember that healing, growth, and transformation are within your reach. You are equipped with the tools and knowledge to effect positive change in your life through EFT tapping. Embrace the journey ahead with confidence, knowing that you hold the power to create the life you desire.

Thank you for allowing me to be a part of your EFT journey. May your path be filled with healing, growth, and abundance.

Your EFT Journey Continues

Thank you for embarking on this journey with EFT tapping through this pocket guide. Your feedback and experiences are invaluable to me and the EFT community. I encourage you to leave a review and share your personal stories about how EFT has impacted your life. Your insights not only help improve future editions of this book but also inspire others to begin their own healing journeys. Together, we can create a supportive and empowering community centered around the transformative power of EFT tapping.

EFT Scripts: Transformative Tapping for Every Journey

These scripts serve as a starting point for your tapping journey, allowing you to customize and tailor your scripting to align with your unique needs and goals.

Energizing Morning Tapping Script:

Start your day with renewed vitality and a positive outlook by engaging in this energizing EFT tapping script. Focus on releasing any lingering fatigue or negativity while infusing yourself with vibrant energy and empowering affirmations. Visualize yourself accomplishing your goals with ease and confidence, ready to tackle whatever challenges may come your way.

Setup Statement While tapping on the Karate Chop point, say:

- Even though I may feel tired or overwhelmed, I choose to tap into my inner strength and vitality now.
- Even though I may feel tired or overwhelmed, I deeply and completely love and accept myself.
- Even though I have challenges ahead, I choose to face them with confidence and enthusiasm.
- Even though I may doubt my abilities, I choose to believe in myself and my capacity to succeed.

Tapping Points:

- **Eyebrow (EB)**: I am ready to embrace this new day with energy and enthusiasm.
- **Side of Eye (SE)**: I release any doubts or fears holding me back.
- **Under Eye (UE)**: I am fully capable of achieving my goals and manifesting my dreams.
- **Under Nose (UN)**: I welcome opportunities for growth and success.

- **Chin (CH)**: I am filled with vibrant energy and vitality.
- **Collarbone (CB)**: I approach challenges with a positive mindset and determination.
- **Under Arm (UA)**: I radiate confidence and enthusiasm in everything I do.
- **Top of Head (TH)**: I am unstoppable in pursuit of my dreams.
- **Eyebrow (EB)**: I am resilient and adaptable, ready to overcome any obstacles.
- **Side of Eye (SE)**: I trust in my ability to navigate challenges with grace and ease.
- **Under Eye (UE)**: I am centered, grounded, and full of energy.
- **Under Nose (UN)**: I embrace the day with open arms and an open heart.
- **Chin (CH)**: I release any tension or stress from my body and mind.
- **Collarbone (CB)**: I am calm, focused, and ready to seize the day.
- **Under Arm (UA)**: I am grateful for the opportunities this day brings.
- **Top of Head (TH)**: I am filled with joy, passion, and purpose.

Take a deep breath and exhale fully. Allow yourself to bask in the energy and positivity you've cultivated through this tapping script. Visualize yourself successfully achieving your goals for the day. See yourself energized, confident, and accomplishing tasks with ease. Affirm your readiness to take on the day with vigor and enthusiasm, knowing that you have the inner resources to manifest your goals and create the life you desire.

Midday Stress Release

Use this EFT tapping script to release the stress and tension that may have built up during the first half of your day. This routine will help you reset and recharge, allowing you to continue your day with renewed energy and a calm mindset.

Setup Statement While tapping on the Karate Chop point, say:

- Even though I feel stressed and overwhelmed right now, I deeply and completely love and accept myself.
- Even though I feel stress building up, I choose to release it now.
- Even though I am overwhelmed by my tasks, I choose to find calm and balance.
- Even though I feel tension in my body, I choose to let it go and relax.

Tapping Points:

- **Eyebrow (EB):** I release the stress and tension from my body and mind.
- **Side of Eye (SE):** I let go of the overwhelm and embrace calmness.
- **Under Eye (UE):** I am releasing any pressure I've put on myself.
- **Under Nose (UN):** I let go of any anxiety about what needs to be done.
- **Chin (CH):** I release the tension in my shoulders and neck.
- **Collarbone (CB):** I am allowing myself to relax and reset.
- **Under Arm (UA):** I choose to feel calm and centered.

- **Top of Head (TH):** I am open to feeling peace and tranquility now.

Second Round of Tapping

- **Eyebrow (EB):** I am capable of handling my tasks with ease.
- **Side of Eye (SE):** I welcome a sense of calm and clarity.
- **Under Eye (UE):** I am letting go of stress and embracing peace.
- **Under Nose (UN):** I choose to stay balanced and grounded.
- **Chin (CH):** I am releasing any negative thoughts or worries.
- **Collarbone (CB):** I am focused and present in this moment.
- **Under Arm (UA):** I trust in my ability to manage my time effectively.
- **Top of Head (TH):** I am recharged and ready to continue my day with calm and confidence.

Take a deep breath and exhale fully. Visualize yourself calmly and efficiently completing your tasks for the rest of the day. Affirm your ability to manage stress and maintain balance, knowing that you can return to this tapping script whenever you need a moment of calm.

Relaxing Evening Routine

As the day comes to a close, it's time to release the stresses and tensions accumulated and invite peace and tranquility into your body and mind. This soothing EFT tapping script will help you transition gracefully from the busyness of the day to a state of relaxation and ease.

Setup Statement While tapping on the Karate Chop point, say:

- Even though I may feel tense or overwhelmed from the day, I deeply and completely love and accept myself.
- Even though I may still carry the stress of the day, I choose to release it now
- Even though my mind may be racing with thoughts, I choose to find peace in this moment.
- Even though I may feel burdened by the day's worries, I choose to let them go and embrace tranquility.

Tapping Points:

- **Eyebrow (EB):** I release the tension from my body and mind, allowing myself to unwind and relax.
- **Side of Eye (SE):** I am calm and at peace within myself.
- **Under Eye (UE):** I invite a sense of calm and serenity into my body and mind.
- **Under Nose (UN):** I am surrounded by peace and tranquility.
- **Chin (CH):** I release any thoughts of the day, allowing my mind to

become quiet and still.

- **Collarbone (CB):** I breathe deeply and slowly, allowing myself to sink into relaxation.
- **Under Arm (UA):** I let go of the worries and concerns of the day, knowing that they can wait until tomorrow.
- **Top of Head (TH):** I am grateful for this moment of peace and relaxation.

Take a deep breath and exhale fully. Allow yourself to sink into the peacefulness and serenity you've cultivated through this tapping script. Feel the tension melting away from your body and mind, leaving you feeling calm, relaxed, and at ease.

Second Round of Tapping

- **Eyebrow (EB):** I let go of the day's stresses and concerns, allowing them to melt away.
- **Side of Eye (SE):** I release any anxieties or worries, allowing myself to fully relax.
- **Under Eye (UE):** I release any tension held in my muscles, allowing them to soften and relax.
- **Under Nose (UN):** I let go of any lingering stress or tension, allowing myself to be present in this moment.
- **Chin (CH):** I am at ease with myself and with the world around me.
- **Collarbone (CB):** I am surrounded by a sense of peace and contentment.
- **Under Arm (UA):** I am safe, supported, and at peace.
- **Top of Head (TH):** I allow myself to fully let go and surrender to the tranquility of the evening.

Take another deep breath and exhale fully. Visualize a specific moment of calm and relaxation, feeling the peace and tranquility wash over you.

Affirm your readiness to embrace the restful night ahead, knowing you have released the tensions of the day.

Healing Past Trauma

Use this EFT tapping script to address and heal past trauma, allowing yourself to release the emotional and physical grip it may have on your present life.
Setup Statement While tapping on the Karate Chop point, say:

- Even though I have experienced deep pain and trauma in the past, I deeply and completely love and accept myself.

Tapping Points

- **Eyebrow (EB):** This pain from my past.
- **Side of Eye (SE):** The memories still haunt me.
- **Under Eye (UE):** I feel it in my body.
- **Under Nose (UN):** It's okay to acknowledge my pain.
- **Chin (CH):** I honor my experiences.
- **Collarbone (CB):** Even though it's hard to face, I'm ready to heal.
- **Under Arm (UA):** Releasing this trauma from my body.
- **Top of Head (TH):** Embracing healing and transformation.

Second Round of Tapping

- **Eyebrow (EB):** I am safe in this moment.
- **Side of Eye (SE):** I release the grip of past trauma.
- **Under Eye (UE):** I am open to healing and peace.
- **Under Nose (UN):** I forgive myself and others involved.

- **Chin (CH):** I am worthy of healing.
- **Collarbone (CB):** I choose to let go of this pain.
- **Under Arm (UA):** I embrace resilience and strength.
- **Top of Head (TH):** I am stepping into a future of healing and wholeness.

Take a deep breath and exhale fully. Visualize yourself moving forward with a sense of peace and resilience, free from the burdens of past trauma. Affirm your readiness to heal and transform, knowing that you have the inner strength to overcome and thrive.

Conquering Anxiety and Fear

Use this EFT tapping script to address and alleviate feelings of anxiety and fear, helping you to find calmness, confidence, and inner peace.

Setup Statement While tapping on the Karate Chop point, say:

- Even though I feel anxious and fearful right now, I deeply and completely love and accept myself.
- Even though my anxiety feels overwhelming, I choose to find peace and calm within.
- Even though fear is holding me back, I choose to release it and embrace confidence.

Tapping Points

- **Eyebrow (EB):** This anxiety I feel.
- **Side of Eye (SE):** This fear in my body.
- **Under Eye (UE):** I feel overwhelmed by anxiety.
- **Under Nose (UN):** It's okay to feel afraid sometimes.
- **Chin (CH):** I acknowledge my anxiety and fear.
- **Collarbone (CB):** I choose to release these anxious feelings.
- **Under Arm (UA):** I am safe and supported.
- **Top of Head (TH):** I allow calmness to wash over me.

Second Round of Tapping

- **Eyebrow (EB):** I am letting go of anxiety.
- **Side of Eye (SE):** I release my fears.
- **Under Eye (UE):** I am calm and centered.
- **Under Nose (UN):** I trust in my ability to handle this.
- **Chin (CH):** I am stronger than my anxiety.
- **Collarbone (CB):** I embrace feelings of peace.
- **Under Arm (UA):** I am confident and secure.
- **Top of Head (TH):** I am free from fear and anxiety.

Take a deep breath and exhale fully. Visualize yourself facing situations with confidence and ease, free from the grip of anxiety and fear. Affirm your ability to remain calm and composed, knowing that you have the inner strength to overcome any challenge.

Overcoming Depression

Use this EFT tapping script to address feelings of sadness and hopelessness, helping you to find light and hope within.

Setup Statement

While tapping on the Karate Chop point, say:

- Even though I feel this overwhelming sadness and hopelessness, I deeply and completely accept myself.
- Even though I feel stuck in this deep, dark cloud, I choose to find a way out and embrace hope.
- Even though it's hard to see the light, I am open to the possibility of feeling better.

Tapping Points

- **Eyebrow (EB):** This heavy sadness.
- **Side of Eye (SE):** This feeling of hopelessness.
- **Under Eye (UE):** I don't know if it will ever go away.
- **Under Nose (UN):** I feel so stuck.
- **Chin (CH):** This deep, dark cloud.
- **Collarbone (CB):** It's so hard to find hope.
- **Under Arm (UA):** But I'm open to the possibility of feeling better.
- **Top of Head (TH):** I choose to find a way out of this darkness.

Second Round of Tapping

- **Eyebrow (EB):** I am open to feeling a little better.
- **Side of Eye (SE):** I release some of this sadness.
- **Under Eye (UE):** I choose to see a glimmer of hope.
- **Under Nose (UN):** I am moving towards the light.
- **Chin (CH):** I release the heaviness in my heart.
- **Collarbone (CB):** I am open to healing.
- **Under Arm (UA):** I am worthy of feeling better.
- **Top of Head (TH):** I embrace the possibility of joy and light.

Take a deep breath and exhale fully. Visualize yourself moving out of the darkness and into the light, feeling the weight lift off your shoulders. Affirm your journey towards healing and embrace the hope that lies ahead.

Building Self-Esteem

Use this EFT tapping script to boost your self-esteem, embrace self-love, and recognize your inherent worth and value. This script will also help you develop a positive self-image, overcome self-doubt, and affirm your self-worth and capabilities.

Setup Statement While tapping on the Karate Chop point, say:

- Even though I struggle with self-esteem, I deeply and completely love and accept myself.
- Even though I sometimes doubt my worth, I choose to see my value and love myself unconditionally.
- Even though I find it hard to believe in myself, I am open to embracing my unique qualities and strengths.

Tapping Points

- **Eyebrow (EB):** I struggle with self-esteem.
- **Side of Eye (SE):** I doubt my worth.
- **Under Eye (UE):** I find it hard to believe in myself.
- **Under Nose (UN):** I feel unworthy at times.
- **Chin (CH):** I release these self-doubts.
- **Collarbone (CB):** I am worthy of love and respect.
- **Under Arm (UA):** I embrace my unique qualities.
- **Top of Head (TH):** I love and accept myself completely.

Second Round of Tapping

- **Eyebrow (EB):** I am confident in my abilities.
- **Side of Eye (SE):** I see my value and worth.
- **Under Eye (UE):** I believe in myself more each day.
- **Under Nose (UN):** I am deserving of success and happiness.
- **Chin (CH):** I embrace self-love and self-acceptance.
- **Collarbone (CB):** I am proud of who I am.
- **Under Arm (UA):** I acknowledge my strengths and talents.
- **Top of Head (TH):** I am enough just as I am.

Third Round of Tapping (for Positive Self-Image and Overcoming Self-Doubt)

- **Eyebrow (EB):** I release negative thoughts about myself.
- **Side of Eye (SE):** I see myself in a positive light.
- **Under Eye (UE):** I overcome self-doubt with confidence.
- **Under Nose (UN):** I trust in my capabilities.
- **Chin (CH):** I am proud of my accomplishments.
- **Collarbone (CB):** I see the good in myself.
- **Under Arm (UA):** I let go of past mistakes.
- **Top of Head (TH):** I embrace my journey and growth.

Affirmations for Self-Worth and Capabilities

- **Eyebrow (EB):** I am worthy of all good things.
- **Side of Eye (SE):** I trust in my abilities.
- **Under Eye (UE):** I am capable of achieving my goals.
- **Under Nose (UN):** I believe in my potential.
- **Chin (CH):** I am strong and resilient.
- **Collarbone (CB):** I value myself and my contributions.

- **Under Arm (UA):** I am confident in who I am.
- **Top of Head (TH):** I love and honor myself completely.

Take a deep breath and exhale fully. Visualize yourself standing tall with confidence, radiating self-love and acceptance. Affirm your worth and the unique qualities that make you who you are.

Managing Anger and Forgiveness

Use these EFT tapping scripts to release anger and embrace forgiveness, both towards yourself and others. These routines will help you let go of negative emotions and cultivate inner peace and understanding.

Tapping Away Anger

Setup Statement While tapping on the Karate Chop point, say:

- Even though I feel this anger burning inside me, I deeply and completely accept myself.
- Even though I am overwhelmed by this anger, I choose to release it now.
- Even though this anger is consuming me, I choose to find calm and peace.

Tapping Points

- **Eyebrow (EB):** This anger.
- **Side of Eye (SE):** Burning inside.
- **Under Eye (UE):** I release this anger.
- **Under Nose (UN):** Letting it go.
- **Chin (CH):** Releasing the tension.
- **Collarbone (CB):** Finding calm.
- **Under Arm (UA):** Letting the anger dissipate.

- **Top of Head (TH):** Feeling peace.

Second Round of Tapping

- **Eyebrow (EB):** I acknowledge my anger.
- **Side of Eye (SE):** I choose to release it.
- **Under Eye (UE):** I am letting go of this burning rage.
- **Under Nose (UN):** I find peace in releasing my anger.
- **Chin (CH):** I am calm and centered.
- **Collarbone (CB):** I embrace tranquility.
- **Under Arm (UA):** I am free from anger.
- **Top of Head (TH):** I choose peace and calm.

Take a deep breath and exhale fully. Visualize yourself feeling calm and at peace, free from the grip of anger.

Forgiveness Scripts

Self-Forgiveness

Setup Statement While tapping on the Karate Chop point, say:

- Even though I struggle to forgive myself for [specific issue], I deeply and completely accept myself.
- Even though I feel guilt and shame, I choose to forgive myself and find peace.
- Even though I am hard on myself, I am open to self-compassion and forgiveness.

Tapping Points

- **Eyebrow (EB):** Struggling to forgive myself.
- **Side of Eye (SE):** This guilt and shame.
- **Under Eye (UE):** I acknowledge my mistakes.
- **Under Nose (UN):** I choose to forgive myself.
- **Chin (CH):** I am worthy of forgiveness.
- **Collarbone (CB):** Letting go of self-judgment.
- **Under Arm (UA):** Embracing self-compassion.
- **Top of Head (TH):** I forgive myself and find peace.

Second Round of Tapping

- **Eyebrow (EB):** I am open to self-forgiveness.
- **Side of Eye (SE):** I release my guilt.
- **Under Eye (UE):** I embrace self-compassion.
- **Under Nose (UN):** I forgive myself for my mistakes.
- **Chin (CH):** I am deserving of love and forgiveness.
- **Collarbone (CB):** I let go of self-judgment.
- **Under Arm (UA):** I am kind to myself.
- **Top of Head (TH):** I am at peace with myself.

Take a deep breath and exhale fully. Visualize yourself embracing self-forgiveness and compassion, feeling lighter and more at peace.

Forgiving Others

Setup Statement While tapping on the Karate Chop point, say:

- Even though I feel resentment towards [person/event], I choose to release this resentment and find peace within myself.
- Even though I am hurt and angry, I am open to the possibility of forgiveness.

- Even though it's hard to let go, I choose to free myself from this resentment.

Tapping Points

- **Eyebrow (EB):** Resentment towards [person/event].
- **Side of Eye (SE):** This hurt and anger.
- **Under Eye (UE):** I acknowledge my pain.
- **Under Nose (UN):** I choose to release this resentment.
- **Chin (CH):** I am open to forgiveness.
- **Collarbone (CB):** Letting go of this burden.
- **Under Arm (UA):** Embracing peace and forgiveness.
- **Top of Head (TH):** I find freedom in forgiving.

Second Round of Tapping

- **Eyebrow (EB):** I release this resentment.
- **Side of Eye (SE):** I choose to forgive.
- **Under Eye (UE):** I let go of my anger.
- **Under Nose (UN):** I find peace in forgiveness.
- **Chin (CH):** I am free from this burden.
- **Collarbone (CB):** I embrace compassion and understanding.
- **Under Arm (UA):** I forgive and release.
- **Top of Head (TH):** I am at peace with myself and others.

Take a deep breath and exhale fully. Visualize yourself letting go of resentment and embracing forgiveness, feeling lighter and more at peace.

Chronic Pain Management

Use this EFT tapping script to manage chronic pain by addressing both the physical sensations and the emotional aspects that may contribute to it. This routine will help you release pain, reduce inflammation, and promote healing in your body.

Setup Statement While tapping on the Karate Chop point, say:

- Even though I feel this chronic pain in my [specific area], I deeply and completely accept myself.
- Even though this pain has been a part of my life for a long time, I choose to release it now.
- Even though I feel frustrated and overwhelmed by this pain, I choose to find relief and healing.

Tapping Points

- **Eyebrow (EB):** This chronic pain in my [specific area].
- **Side of Eye (SE):** This persistent discomfort.
- **Under Eye (UE):** I acknowledge the pain I feel.
- **Under Nose (UN):** It's hard to manage this pain daily.
- **Chin (CH):** I feel so tired of this constant pain.
- **Collarbone (CB):** I choose to release this pain now.
- **Under Arm (UA):** I am open to healing.
- **Top of Head (TH):** I embrace relief and comfort.

Second Round of Tapping

- **Eyebrow (EB):** I release the tension in my [specific area].
- **Side of Eye (SE):** I let go of the inflammation and discomfort.
- **Under Eye (UE):** I choose to feel at ease in my body.
- **Under Nose (UN):** I allow my body to heal.
- **Chin (CH):** I trust in my body's ability to recover.
- **Collarbone (CB):** I am open to experiencing pain-free days.
- **Under Arm (UA):** I embrace healing and well-being.
- **Top of Head (TH):** I am free from chronic pain.

Visualization and Affirmations

While continuing to tap through the points, visualize yourself moving freely and comfortably, without pain. Imagine your body as healthy and strong, capable of healing itself.

- **Eyebrow (EB):** I see myself free from pain.
- **Side of Eye (SE):** I am active and vibrant.
- **Under Eye (UE):** My body heals itself naturally.
- **Under Nose (UN):** I am grateful for my body's resilience.
- **Chin (CH):** I trust in my body's healing process.
- **Collarbone (CB):** I am surrounded by healing energy.
- **Under Arm (UA):** I embrace a pain-free life.
- **Top of Head (TH):** I am healthy, strong, and whole.

Take a deep breath and exhale fully. Visualize yourself living a life free from chronic pain, embracing health and vitality. Affirm your commitment to healing and well-being, knowing that you have the power to influence your body's ability to recover.

Weight Loss and Emotional Eating

Emotional Triggers and Stress Eating

Purpose: Address the emotional reasons behind eating habits and stress-induced eating.

Setup Statement While tapping on the Karate Chop point, say:

- Even though I feel [specific emotion, e.g., stressed] and it makes me want to eat, I deeply and completely accept myself.
- Even though I reach for food when I'm feeling [specific emotion], I choose to understand and address this emotion.
- Even though I use food to cope with [specific emotion], I am open to finding healthier ways to deal with it.

Tapping Points

- **Eyebrow (EB):** This [specific emotion] makes me want to eat.
- **Side of Eye (SE):** I feel this urge to eat whenever I'm [specific emotion].
- **Under Eye (UE):** I don't want to feel this way.
- **Under Nose (UN):** It's hard to control my eating when I'm [specific emotion].
- **Chin (CH):** I use food to cope with [specific emotion].
- **Collarbone (CB):** This [specific emotion] is overwhelming.

- **Under Arm (UA):** I feel out of control when I'm [specific emotion].
- **Top of Head (TH):** I'm ready to address this [specific emotion] in a healthy way.

Second Round of Tapping

- **Eyebrow (EB):** I acknowledge this [specific emotion].
- **Side of Eye (SE):** I understand why I turn to food.
- **Under Eye (UE):** I choose to find healthier ways to cope.
- **Under Nose (UN):** I am in control of my emotions.
- **Chin (CH):** I release the need to eat when I'm [specific emotion].
- **Collarbone (CB):** I am open to healthier coping mechanisms.
- **Under Arm (UA):** I choose to manage my emotions without food.
- **Top of Head (TH):** I am calm and in control.

Cravings and Overeating

Purpose: Address the cravings that lead to overeating.

Setup Statement While tapping on the Karate Chop point, say:

- Even though I crave [specific food], I deeply and completely accept myself.
- Even though I feel an intense craving for [specific food], I choose to understand and control it.
- Even though I use [specific food] to feel better, I am open to finding healthier ways to satisfy myself.

Tapping Points

- **Eyebrow (EB):** This craving for [specific food].
- **Side of Eye (SE):** I feel this craving strongly.

154

- **Under Eye (UE):** I don't want to feel controlled by this craving.
- **Under Nose (UN):** It's hard to resist [specific food].
- **Chin (CH):** I use [specific food] to cope with my emotions.
- **Collarbone (CB):** This craving is overwhelming.
- **Under Arm (UA):** I feel out of control around [specific food].
- **Top of Head (TH):** I'm ready to address this craving in a healthy way.

Second Round of Tapping

- **Eyebrow (EB):** I acknowledge this craving.
- **Side of Eye (SE):** I understand why I crave [specific food].
- **Under Eye (UE):** I choose to find healthier ways to cope.
- **Under Nose (UN):** I am in control of my cravings.
- **Chin (CH):** I release the need for [specific food].
- **Collarbone (CB):** I am open to healthier choices.
- **Under Arm (UA):** I choose to manage my cravings.
- **Top of Head (TH):** I am calm and in control.

Body Image and Self-Acceptance

Purpose: Foster a positive body image and self-acceptance, which is crucial for sustainable weight loss.

Setup Statement While tapping on the Karate Chop point, say:

- Even though I struggle with my body image, I deeply and completely accept myself.
- Even though I don't always feel positive about my body, I choose to love and accept myself.
- Even though I have negative thoughts about my body, I am open to seeing myself with kindness and compassion.

Tapping Points

- **Eyebrow (EB):** I struggle with my body image.
- **Side of Eye (SE):** I don't always feel positive about my body.
- **Under Eye (UE):** I have negative thoughts about my appearance.
- **Under Nose (UN):** It's hard to accept myself as I am.
- **Chin (CH):** I want to love and accept myself.
- **Collarbone (CB):** I am learning to see myself with kindness.
- **Under Arm (UA):** I choose to embrace my body.
- **Top of Head (TH):** I am worthy of love and acceptance.

Second Round of Tapping

- **Eyebrow (EB):** I release my negative thoughts about my body.
- **Side of Eye (SE):** I am open to seeing myself with compassion.
- **Under Eye (UE):** I choose to love and accept myself.
- **Under Nose (UN):** I appreciate my body for all it does.
- **Chin (CH):** I am learning to love myself more each day.
- **Collarbone (CB):** I embrace my body as it is.
- **Under Arm (UA):** I am worthy of self-love and acceptance.
- **Top of Head (TH):** I see myself with kindness and compassion.

Emotional Eating and Finding Balance

Purpose: Help individuals find balance and develop healthier eating habits.

Setup Statement While tapping on the Karate Chop point, say:

- Even though I turn to food for comfort, I deeply and completely accept myself.
- Even though I eat when I'm not hungry, I choose to find balance

and listen to my body.
- Even though I have used food to cope with emotions, I am open to finding healthier ways to nourish myself.

Tapping Points

- **Eyebrow (EB):** I turn to food for comfort.
- **Side of Eye (SE):** I eat when I'm not hungry.
- **Under Eye (UE):** I use food to cope with my emotions.
- **Under Nose (UN):** It's hard to find balance.
- **Chin (CH):** I want to listen to my body.
- **Collarbone (CB):** I am open to healthier ways to cope.
- **Under Arm (UA):** I choose to nourish myself in healthy ways.
- **Top of Head (TH):** I am finding balance in my eating habits.

Second Round of Tapping

- **Eyebrow (EB):** I acknowledge my emotional eating.
- **Side of Eye (SE):** I am learning to listen to my body.
- **Under Eye (UE):** I choose healthier ways to cope.
- **Under Nose (UN):** I find balance in my eating.
- **Chin (CH):** I nourish myself with love and care.
- **Collarbone (CB):** I am open to positive changes.
- **Under Arm (UA):** I choose balance and health.
- **Top of Head (TH):** I am in control of my eating habits.

Take a deep breath and exhale fully. Visualize yourself making healthy food choices and feeling balanced and in control. Affirm your commitment to nourishing your body and mind with love and care.

Comprehensive Sleep Improvement Tapping Script

This EFT tapping script is designed to help you achieve a peaceful and restful night's sleep by addressing various factors that contribute to insomnia. Use this script to calm your mind, release anxiety, and create an environment conducive to sleep.

Setup Statement While tapping on the Karate Chop point, say:

- Even though I have difficulty sleeping, I deeply and completely accept myself and choose to create a peaceful and restful sleep experience.
- Even though my mind is busy and I find it hard to relax, I choose to release these thoughts and embrace calmness.
- Even though I feel anxious about not sleeping well, I choose to let go of this anxiety and trust in my ability to rest.

Tapping Points:

- **Eyebrow (EB):** I struggle with sleep.
- **Side of Eye (SE):** I want to sleep better.
- **Under Eye (UE):** I need to calm my mind and body.
- **Under Nose (UN):** I'm working on my sleep habits.
- **Chin (CH):** I deserve a good night's sleep.
- **Collarbone (CB):** I'm making changes to improve my sleep.

- **Under Arm (UA):** I'm creating a sleep-friendly environment.
- **Top of Head (TH):** I am ready to sleep peacefully and deeply.

Second Round of Tapping:

- **Eyebrow (EB):** I release the stress and tension from my body and mind.
- **Side of Eye (SE):** I let go of the overwhelm and embrace calmness.
- **Under Eye (UE):** I am releasing any pressure I've put on myself.
- **Under Nose (UN):** I let go of any anxiety about what needs to be done.
- **Chin (CH):** I release the tension in my shoulders and neck.
- **Collarbone (CB):** I am allowing myself to relax and reset.
- **Under Arm (UA):** I choose to feel calm and centered.
- **Top of Head (TH):** I am open to feeling peace and tranquility now.

Closing Visualization

Take a deep breath and exhale fully. Visualize yourself in a calm and serene environment, feeling completely relaxed and ready for a deep, restful sleep. Affirm your readiness to release any remaining stress and embrace the peacefulness of the night.

Boosting Energy Levels

Morning Energy Boost

Start your day with renewed vitality and a positive outlook by engaging in this energizing EFT tapping script. As you tap on each meridian point, focus on releasing any lingering fatigue or negativity while infusing yourself with vibrant energy and empowering affirmations.

Setup Statement While tapping on the Karate Chop point, say:

- Even though I feel tired and sluggish, I deeply and completely accept myself.
- Even though it's hard to find the energy to start the day, I choose to release this fatigue and welcome vitality.
- Even though I feel drained and exhausted, I am open to feeling more awake and alert.

Tapping Points:

- **Eyebrow (EB):** This fatigue is weighing me down.
- **Side of Eye (SE):** It's hard to find the energy to start the day.
- **Under Eye (UE):** I feel drained and exhausted.
- **Under Nose (UN):** But I choose to release this fatigue.
- **Chin (CH):** I welcome vitality into my body.
- **Collarbone (CB):** I am open to feeling more awake and alert.

- **Under Arm (UA):** Feeling energized and refreshed.
- **Top of Head (TH):** I am ready to embrace the day with renewed energy.

Second Round of Tapping:

- **Eyebrow (EB):** I release the fatigue from my body.
- **Side of Eye (SE):** I embrace a sense of vitality and energy.
- **Under Eye (UE):** I feel more awake and alert.
- **Under Nose (UN):** I am energized and refreshed.
- **Chin (CH):** I am filled with vibrant energy.
- **Collarbone (CB):** I am ready to take on the day.
- **Under Arm (UA):** I feel revitalized and alive.
- **Top of Head (TH):** I embrace the day with enthusiasm and joy.

Closing Visualization

Take a deep breath and exhale fully. Visualize yourself accomplishing your goals with ease and confidence, ready to tackle whatever challenges may come your way.

Midday Rejuvenation

Use this EFT tapping script to release the stress and tension that may have built up during the first half of your day. This routine will help you reset and recharge, allowing you to continue your day with renewed energy and a calm mindset.

Setup Statement While tapping on the Karate Chop point, say:

- Even though I feel a slump in my energy, I deeply and completely accept myself.
- Even though this midday fatigue is overwhelming, I choose to

rejuvenate my energy.

- Even though I feel like I'm running on empty, I am revitalized and energized.

Tapping Points:

- **Eyebrow (EB):** This midday fatigue is overwhelming.
- **Side of Eye (SE):** I feel like I'm running on empty.
- **Under Eye (UE):** But I choose to rejuvenate my energy.
- **Under Nose (UN):** Releasing all tiredness and fatigue.
- **Chin (CH):** I am revitalized and energized.
- **Collarbone (CB):** My energy is returning.
- **Under Arm (UA):** Feeling refreshed and invigorated.
- **Top of Head (TH):** I am filled with renewed energy and vitality.

Second Round of Tapping:

- **Eyebrow (EB):** I release the midday slump.
- **Side of Eye (SE):** I welcome a surge of energy.
- **Under Eye (UE):** I feel rejuvenated and alert.
- **Under Nose (UN):** I am revitalized and focused.
- **Chin (CH):** My energy is restored.
- **Collarbone (CB):** I am ready to continue my day with enthusiasm.
- **Under Arm (UA):** I feel vibrant and alive.
- **Top of Head (TH):** I embrace the rest of the day with renewed vigor.

Closing Visualization

Take a deep breath and exhale fully. Visualize yourself completing the rest of your tasks with energy and focus, feeling recharged and invigorated.

Clearing Financial Blockages and Embracing Abundance

Releasing Limiting Beliefs About Money

Setup Statement While tapping on the Karate Chop point, say:

- Even though I believe money is hard to come by, I deeply and completely accept myself.
- Even though I think I'll never have enough money, I choose to release this belief and open myself to abundance.

Tapping Points:

- **Eyebrow (EB):** This belief that money is hard to come by.
- **Side of Eye (SE):** The fear that I'll never have enough money.
- **Under Eye (UE):** The feeling of scarcity and lack.
- **Under Nose (UN):** All these limiting beliefs about money.
- **Chin (CH):** I release these negative beliefs about money.
- **Collarbone (CB):** I am open to new opportunities for financial abundance.
- **Under Arm (UA):** I am worthy of financial success and abundance.
- **Top of Head (TH):** I welcome financial abundance and prosperity.

Overcoming Fear of Financial Failure

Setup Statement While tapping on the Karate Chop point, say:

- Even though I'm afraid of financial failure, I deeply and completely accept myself.
- Even though I worry about making poor financial decisions, I choose to trust in my ability to manage money wisely.

Tapping Points:

- **Eyebrow (EB):** This fear of financial failure.
- **Side of Eye (SE):** Worrying about making poor financial decisions.
- **Under Eye (UE):** The anxiety about never achieving financial stability.
- **Under Nose (UN):** All this fear around money.
- **Chin (CH):** The doubts about my financial abilities.
- **Collarbone (CB):** I release these fears and doubts.
- **Under Arm (UA):** I trust in my ability to manage money wisely.
- **Top of Head (TH):** I am confident in my financial decisions and open to abundance.

Embracing Financial Abundance

Setup Statement While tapping on the Karate Chop point, say:

- Even though I have struggled with money in the past, I choose to embrace financial abundance now.
- Even though I've felt undeserving of wealth, I am ready to attract abundance into my life.

Tapping Points:

- **Eyebrow (EB):** I have struggled with money in the past.
- **Side of Eye (SE):** Feeling undeserving of wealth.
- **Under Eye (UE):** This scarcity mindset.
- **Under Nose (UN):** I choose to embrace financial abundance.
- **Chin (CH):** I am ready to attract wealth into my life.
- **Collarbone (CB):** I am deserving of financial success.
- **Under Arm (UA):** I release the scarcity mindset.
- **Top of Head (TH):** I welcome financial abundance and prosperity.

Visualizing and Manifesting Financial Goals

Setup Statement While tapping on the Karate Chop point, say:

- Even though I've struggled to see myself as financially successful, I choose to visualize my abundant future now.

Tapping Points:

- **Eyebrow (EB):** I have struggled to see myself as financially successful.
- **Side of Eye (SE):** Finding it hard to imagine wealth.
- **Under Eye (UE):** Doubting my ability to attract money.
- **Under Nose (UN):** I choose to visualize my abundant future.
- **Chin (CH):** I am ready to manifest my financial goals.
- **Collarbone (CB):** I believe in my potential to attract wealth.
- **Under Arm (UA):** I see myself as financially successful.
- **Top of Head (TH):** I manifest my financial goals with each tap.

Practicing Gratitude for Abundance

Setup Statement While tapping on the Karate Chop point, say:

- Even though I sometimes focus on what I lack, I choose to focus on the abundance I already have.

Tapping Points:

- **Eyebrow (EB):** I sometimes focus on what I lack.
- **Side of Eye (SE):** Forgetting to be grateful.
- **Under Eye (UE):** Overlooking the abundance around me.
- **Under Nose (UN):** I choose to focus on the abundance I already have.
- **Chin (CH):** I am ready to cultivate a mindset of gratitude.
- **Collarbone (CB):** I appreciate all the wealth in my life.
- **Under Arm (UA):** I am grateful for the financial abundance I experience.

Top of Head (TH): I embrace gratitude and attract even more abundance.

Enhancing Relationships

Use this EFT tapping script to address relationship challenges, enhance empathy and understanding, heal past traumas, and cultivate love and connection. This routine will help you build stronger, healthier, and more fulfilling relationships.

Setup Statement While tapping on the Karate Chop point, say:

- Even though I struggle with [specific relationship challenge], I deeply and completely accept myself.
- Even though I feel [emotion] when dealing with [relationship issue], I choose to find peace and understanding.
- Even though past wounds still hurt, I am open to healing and building meaningful connections.

Tapping Points:

- **Eyebrow (EB):** Struggling with [specific relationship challenge].
- **Side of Eye (SE):** Feeling [emotion] about this issue.
- **Under Eye (UE):** This tension in my relationship.
- **Under Nose (UN):** Worrying about [relationship challenge].
- **Chin (CH):** Feeling stressed and upset.
- **Collarbone (CB):** This ongoing conflict.
- **Under Arm (UA):** I want to resolve this peacefully.
- **Top of Head (TH):** I choose to find understanding and harmony.

Second Round of Tapping:

- **Eyebrow (EB):** Pain from past relationships.
- **Side of Eye (SE):** These old wounds still hurt.
- **Under Eye (UE):** Fear of opening up again.
- **Under Nose (UN):** Feeling stuck in past pain.
- **Chin (CH):** Worrying about being hurt again.
- **Collarbone (CB):** This lingering relationship trauma.
- **Under Arm (UA):** I want to release this pain.
- **Top of Head (TH):** I choose to heal and move forward.

Third Round of Tapping:

- **Eyebrow (EB):** I am worthy of love and connection.
- **Side of Eye (SE):** I attract healthy, loving relationships.
- **Under Eye (UE):** I am open to deep connections.
- **Under Nose (UN):** I give and receive love freely.
- **Chin (CH):** I nurture my relationships with care.
- **Collarbone (CB):** I embrace empathy and understanding.
- **Under Arm (UA):** I am a source of love and positivity.
- **Top of Head (TH):** I cultivate loving and meaningful connections.

Take a deep breath and exhale fully. Visualize yourself experiencing fulfilling and harmonious relationships. Affirm your ability to build and maintain strong connections, knowing that you can return to this tapping script whenever you need to enhance your relationships.

Chakra Balancing Tapping Scripts

Root Chakra (Muladhara)

Setup Statement While tapping on the Karate Chop point, say:

- Even though I may feel disconnected or insecure, I deeply and completely accept myself.
- Even though I feel ungrounded and fearful, I choose to feel safe and supported.
- Even though I lack stability, I am open to embracing security and grounding.

Tapping Points:

- **Eyebrow (EB):** Feeling ungrounded.
- **Side of Eye (SE):** Insecurity and fear.
- **Under Eye (UE):** Lack of stability.
- **Under Nose (UN):** Feeling disconnected.
- **Chin (CH):** I release fear and insecurity.
- **Collarbone (CB):** I am safe and supported.
- **Under Arm (UA):** I trust in the abundance of the universe.
- **Top of Head (TH):** I am rooted and secure.

Sacral Chakra (Swadhisthana)

Setup Statement While tapping on the Karate Chop point, say:

- Even though I may struggle with my emotions and creativity, I deeply and completely accept myself.
- Even though I feel emotionally blocked, I choose to embrace my emotions.
- Even though I fear change, I am open to creative flow and passion.

Tapping Points:

- **Eyebrow (EB):** Emotional blockages.
- **Side of Eye (SE):** Creative stagnation.
- **Under Eye (UE):** Fear of change.
- **Under Nose (UN):** I release emotional resistance.
- **Chin (CH):** I embrace my creativity.
- **Collarbone (CB):** I allow my emotions to flow.
- **Under Arm (UA):** I am passionate and creative.
- **Top of Head (TH):** I am in touch with my emotions and creativity.

Solar Plexus Chakra (Manipura)

Setup Statement While tapping on the Karate Chop point, say:

- Even though I may struggle with self-esteem and personal power, I deeply and completely accept myself.
- Even though I doubt my abilities, I choose to feel confident and empowered.
- Even though I feel powerless, I am open to embracing my inner strength.

Tapping Points:

- **Eyebrow (EB):** Low self-esteem.
- **Side of Eye (SE):** Feeling powerless.
- **Under Eye (UE):** Self-doubt.
- **Under Nose (UN):** I release self-limiting beliefs.
- **Chin (CH):** I embrace my personal power.
- **Collarbone (CB):** I trust in my inner wisdom.
- **Under Arm (UA):** I am confident and empowered.
- **Top of Head (TH):** I am worthy of success and abundance.

Heart Chakra (Anahata)

Setup Statement While tapping on the Karate Chop point, say:

- Even though I may struggle with giving and receiving love, I deeply and completely accept myself.
- Even though I fear rejection, I choose to open my heart to love.
- Even though I find it hard to forgive, I am open to healing my heart.

Tapping Points:

- **Eyebrow (EB):** Closed heart.
- **Side of Eye (SE):** Fear of rejection.
- **Under Eye (UE):** Difficulty in forgiving.
- **Under Nose (UN):** I release past hurts.
- **Chin (CH):** I open my heart to love.
- **Collarbone (CB):** I am worthy of love and connection.
- **Under Arm (UA):** I give and receive love freely.
- **Top of Head (TH):** I am filled with love and compassion.

Throat Chakra (Vishuddha)

Setup Statement While tapping on the Karate Chop point, say:

- Even though I may struggle with communication and self-expression, I deeply and completely accept myself.
- Even though I fear speaking my truth, I choose to express myself freely.
- Even though I feel unheard, I am open to clear and confident communication.

Tapping Points:

- **Eyebrow (EB):** Blocked communication.
- **Side of Eye (SE):** Fear of speaking up.
- **Under Eye (UE):** Feeling unheard.
- **Under Nose (UN):** I release communication barriers.
- **Chin (CH):** I speak my truth with confidence.
- **Collarbone (CB):** I express myself freely.
- **Under Arm (UA):** I am a clear and effective communicator.
- **Top of Head (TH):** My voice matters and is heard.

Third Eye Chakra (Ajna)

Setup Statement While tapping on the Karate Chop point, say:

- Even though I may struggle with intuition and clarity, I deeply and completely accept myself.
- Even though I doubt my inner wisdom, I choose to trust my intuition.
- Even though I feel confused, I am open to seeing clearly.

Tapping Points:

- **Eyebrow (EB):** Blocked intuition.
- **Side of Eye (SE):** Confusion and indecision.
- **Under Eye (UE):** Lack of clarity.
- **Under Nose (UN):** I release mental fog.
- **Chin (CH):** I trust my inner wisdom.
- **Collarbone (CB):** I see clearly and intuitively.
- **Under Arm (UA):** I am connected to my higher self.
- **Top of Head (TH):** I trust the guidance of my intuition.

Crown Chakra (Sahasrara)

Setup Statement While tapping on the Karate Chop point, say:

- Even though I may feel disconnected from divine wisdom and higher consciousness, I deeply and completely accept myself.
- Even though I feel spiritually adrift, I choose to embrace spiritual connection.
- Even though I lack spiritual connection, I am open to divine guidance.

Tapping Points:

- **Eyebrow (EB):** Disconnected from higher consciousness.
- **Side of Eye (SE):** Feeling spiritually adrift.
- **Under Eye (UE):** Lack of spiritual connection.
- **Under Nose (UN):** I release spiritual blockages.
- **Chin (CH):** I am connected to universal wisdom.
- **Collarbone (CB):** I am one with the universe.
- **Under Arm (UA):** I am aligned with divine guidance.

- **Top of Head (TH):** I am open to receiving divine inspiration.

These tapping scripts are designed to clear and balance each Chakra, promoting vitality, alignment, and harmony within the Chakra system.

Enhancing Intuition

Use these EFT tapping scripts to strengthen your intuitive abilities and trust your inner guidance. These routines will help you release doubts and fears, enabling you to connect more deeply with your intuition.

Setup Statement: While tapping on the Karate Chop point, say:

- Even though I struggle to trust my intuition, I deeply and completely accept myself.
- Even though I doubt my intuitive abilities, I choose to release these doubts and embrace my inner wisdom.
- Even though I fear making wrong decisions based on my intuition, I deeply and completely accept who I am.

Tapping Points:
First Round:

- **Eyebrow (EB):** I doubt my intuition.
- **Side of Eye (SE):** I fear making wrong decisions.
- **Under Eye (UE):** Past experiences cloud my intuition.
- **Under Nose (UN):** I release fear and doubt.
- **Chin (CH):** I trust my inner wisdom.
- **Collarbone (CB):** My intuition guides me wisely.
- **Under Arm (UA):** I am open to receiving intuitive insights.
- **Top of Head (TH):** I trust and honor my intuition.

Second Round:

- **Eyebrow (EB):** I release any blocks to my intuition.
- **Side of Eye (SE):** I am calm and centered.
- **Under Eye (UE):** My mind is quiet, and my heart is open.
- **Under Nose (UN):** I hear my inner voice clearly.
- **Chin (CH):** I act on my intuition with confidence.
- **Collarbone (CB):** I am connected to my inner guidance.
- **Under Arm (UA):** Intuitive wisdom flows through me easily.
- **Top of Head (TH):** I trust the messages I receive.

Closing Statement: Take a deep breath and exhale fully. Visualize yourself confidently receiving and following intuitive guidance, feeling assured and at peace with the wisdom that flows from within.

Manifesting Dreams

Use these EFT tapping scripts to align your energy with your goals and dreams, creating a powerful mindset for manifestation.

Manifesting Financial Abundance:

Setup Statement: While tapping on the Karate Chop point, say:

- Even though I believe I'm not worthy of abundance, I deeply and completely accept myself.

Tapping Points:

- **Eyebrow (EB):** I release my fears around abundance.
- **Side of Eye (SE):** I attract financial prosperity.
- **Under Eye (UE):** I am open to receiving abundance.
- **Under Nose (UN):** Abundance flows to me easily.
- **Chin (CH):** I am worthy of financial success.
- **Collarbone (CB):** I trust in my ability to create wealth.
- **Under Arm (UA):** I embrace abundance in all forms.
- **Top of Head (TH):** I manifest financial prosperity.

Manifesting Love and Relationships:

Setup Statement: While tapping on the Karate Chop point, say:

- Even though I feel unlovable, I deeply and completely accept myself.

Tapping Points:

- **Eyebrow (EB):** I release my fears around love.
- **Side of Eye (SE):** I attract a loving relationship.
- **Under Eye (UE):** I am open to receiving love.
- **Under Nose (UN):** Love flows to me easily.
- **Chin (CH):** I am worthy of love.
- **Collarbone (CB):** I trust in my ability to find love.
- **Under Arm (UA):** I embrace love in all forms.
- **Top of Head (TH):** I manifest a loving relationship.

Manifesting Career Success:

Setup Statement: While tapping on the Karate Chop point, say:

- Even though I doubt my abilities, I deeply and completely accept myself.

Tapping Points:

- **Eyebrow (EB):** I release my fears about my career.
- **Side of Eye (SE):** I attract career opportunities.
- **Under Eye (UE):** I am open to professional growth.
- **Under Nose (UN):** Success flows to me easily.
- **Chin (CH):** I am worthy of professional success.

- **Collarbone (CB):** I trust in my career path.
- **Under Arm (UA):** I embrace career growth in all forms.
- **Top of Head (TH):** I manifest professional success.

Manifesting Health and Wellness:

Setup Statement: While tapping on the Karate Chop point, say:

- Even though I struggle with my health, I deeply and completely accept myself.

Tapping Points:

- **Eyebrow (EB):** I release my fears about my health.
- **Side of Eye (SE):** I attract vibrant health.
- **Under Eye (UE):** I am open to healing.
- **Under Nose (UN):** Health flows to me easily.
- **Chin (CH):** I am worthy of good health.
- **Collarbone (CB):** I trust in my body's ability to heal.
- **Under Arm (UA):** I embrace wellness in all forms.
- **Top of Head (TH):** I manifest vibrant health.

Manifesting Personal Growth:

Setup Statement: While tapping on the Karate Chop point, say:

- Even though I feel stuck in my personal growth, I deeply and completely accept myself.

Tapping Points:

- **Eyebrow (EB):** I release my fears about personal growth.
- **Side of Eye (SE):** I attract growth opportunities.
- **Under Eye (UE):** I am open to personal transformation.
- **Under Nose (UN):** Growth flows to me easily.
- **Chin (CH):** I am worthy of personal development.
- **Collarbone (CB):** I trust in my journey of growth.
- **Under Arm (UA):** I embrace transformation in all forms.
- **Top of Head (TH):** I manifest personal growth.

Closing Statement: Take a deep breath and exhale fully. Visualize yourself achieving these goals with ease and confidence, knowing that you are capable of manifesting your dreams into reality.

Cultivating Gratitude Tapping Script

Use this EFT tapping script to cultivate a daily gratitude practice, overcome resistance to gratitude, and find gratitude even in challenging times. This routine will help you shift your perception towards positivity and enhance your overall well-being.

Setup Statement While tapping on the Karate Chop point, say:

- Even though I sometimes forget to be grateful, I deeply and completely accept myself.
- Even though I struggle to find things to be grateful for, I deeply and completely accept myself.
- Even though I sometimes focus on the negative, I choose to appreciate the good in my life.

Tapping Points and Reminder Phrases:

- **Eyebrow (EB):** I am grateful for this moment.
- **Side of Eye (SE):** I appreciate the small joys in my life.
- **Under Eye (UE):** I am thankful for the love around me.
- **Under Nose (UN):** I recognize the abundance I have.
- **Chin (CH):** I am grateful for my health.
- **Collarbone (CB):** I appreciate my abilities and talents.
- **Under Arm (UA):** I am thankful for my relationships.
- **Top of Head (TH):** I am grateful for the opportunities I have.

Second Round of Tapping

- **Eyebrow (EB):** I feel resistant to gratitude.
- **Side of Eye (SE):** It's hard to see the good.
- **Under Eye (UE):** I feel negative about my life.
- **Under Nose (UN):** This resistance to being grateful.
- **Chin (CH):** These negative thoughts.
- **Collarbone (CB):** I am open to changing my perspective.
- **Under Arm (UA):** I choose to see the good.
- **Top of Head (TH):** I allow myself to feel grateful.

Third Round of Tapping

- **Eyebrow (EB):** These challenging times.
- **Side of Eye (SE):** It's hard to feel grateful.
- **Under Eye (UE):** I feel overwhelmed.
- **Under Nose (UN):** This sense of struggle.
- **Chin (CH):** I choose to find gratitude.
- **Collarbone (CB):** I appreciate the small things.
- **Under Arm (UA):** I am grateful for moments of peace.
- **Top of Head (TH):** I choose to see the good even now.

Closing Statement: Take a deep breath and exhale fully. Reflect on the gratitude you have cultivated through this tapping script. Feel the positive shift in your perception and embrace the sense of peace and well-being it brings. Remember, you can return to this tapping script whenever you need to reconnect with gratitude.

Creating Custom Tapping Scripts for Gratitude

Identify the Focus: Determine the specific area or aspect of gratitude you wish to enhance (e.g., health, relationships, career).

Setup Statements: Craft three setup statements addressing any resistance or negative feelings about the focus area. Example:

- Even though I struggle to appreciate my job, I deeply and completely accept myself.
- Even though I sometimes feel unappreciated in my relationships, I deeply and completely accept myself.
- Even though I find it hard to be grateful for my current health condition, I choose to find small things to appreciate.

Tapping Points and Affirmations: Develop affirmations that reflect positive shifts related to the focus area. Example:

- **Eyebrow (EB):** I am grateful for the stability my job provides.
- **Side of Eye (SE):** I appreciate the love and support in my relationships.
- **Under Eye (UE):** I am thankful for the strength and resilience of my body.
- **Under Nose (UN):** I recognize the abundance in my career.
- **Chin (CH):** I am grateful for the connection with my loved ones.
- **Collarbone (CB):** I appreciate my health and well-being.
- **Under Arm (UA):** I am thankful for my professional growth.
- **Top of Head (TH):** I embrace gratitude for the love and care in my life.

Repeat and Adjust: Repeat the tapping script multiple times, making adjustments based on how you feel after each round. Focus on deepening your sense of gratitude and noticing any shifts in your feelings.

Example Custom Gratitude Script

Focus: Gratitude for Health
   Setup Statements:

- Even though I struggle to appreciate my current health condition, I deeply and completely accept myself.
- Even though I feel frustrated with my body, I choose to find small things to appreciate.
- Even though I sometimes focus on my health challenges, I choose to see the good in my body.

Tapping Points and Affirmations:

- **Eyebrow (EB):** I am grateful for the strength in my body.
- **Side of Eye (SE):** I appreciate my body's resilience.
- **Under Eye (UE):** I am thankful for the health I have.
- **Under Nose (UN):** I recognize the small victories in my health journey.
- **Chin (CH):** I am grateful for my body's ability to heal.
- **Collarbone (CB):** I appreciate the support I receive for my health.
- **Under Arm (UA):** I am thankful for my body's endurance.
- **Top of Head (TH):** I embrace gratitude for my health and well-being.

Spiritual Connection Tapping Scripts

Enhancing Spiritual Connection

To foster a deeper sense of connection with the universe and higher self, promoting feelings of oneness, peace, and clarity.

Setup Statement: While tapping on the Karate Chop point, say:

- Even though I feel disconnected from the universe, I deeply and completely accept myself and am open to experiencing oneness.
- Even though I sometimes struggle to feel love and peace, I deeply and completely accept myself and am open to higher frequencies of love, peace, and oneness.
- Even though I sometimes feel disconnected from my higher self, I deeply and completely accept myself and am open to connecting with my higher self.

Tapping Script:

- **Eyebrow (EB):** I release my sense of isolation.
- **Side of Eye (SE):** I open myself to universal love.
- **Under Eye (UE):** I am connected to all that is.
- **Under Nose (UN):** I feel the presence of my higher self.
- **Chin (CH):** I trust in the wisdom of the universe.
- **Collarbone (CB):** I am one with the cosmos.

- **Under Arm (UA):** I embrace my spiritual connection.
- **Top of Head (TH):** I am a part of the infinite universe.

Additional Rounds:

- **EB:** I release any doubts about my intuition.
- **SE:** I am open to receiving guidance.
- **UE:** I trust in my inner wisdom.
- **UN:** I am a clear channel for divine messages.
- **CH:** I receive guidance with clarity and ease.
- **CB:** I trust the messages from my higher self.
- **UA:** I am aligned with divine wisdom.
- **TH:** I am open and receptive to guidance.

Accessing Inner Wisdom and Soul's Purpose

To access ancient wisdom and align with your soul's purpose, enhancing spiritual growth and clarity.

Setup Statement: While tapping on the Karate Chop point, say:

- Even though I sometimes doubt my ability to access ancient wisdom, I deeply and completely accept myself and am open to discovering my soul's purpose.
- Even though I doubt my ability to receive guidance, I deeply and completely accept myself and am open to becoming a clear channel for divine guidance.
- Even though I feel disconnected from divine wisdom and higher consciousness, I deeply and completely accept myself.

Tapping Script:

- **Eyebrow (EB):** I release my doubts about my soul's purpose.
- **Side of Eye (SE):** I am open to ancient wisdom.
- **Under Eye (UE):** I trust the knowledge within me.
- **Under Nose (UN):** I am connected to my soul's purpose.
- **Chin (CH):** I receive guidance from ancient wisdom.
- **Collarbone (CB):** I align with my soul's mission.
- **Under Arm (UA):** I embrace my spiritual journey.
- **Top of Head (TH):** I am guided by my soul's purpose.

Additional Rounds:

- **EB:** I release my doubts about my higher self.
- **SE:** I am in tune with my higher self.
- **UE:** I receive guidance clearly.
- **UN:** I trust my inner wisdom.
- **CH:** I am aligned with my higher self.
- **CB:** I am connected to my true self.
- **UA:** I embrace my spiritual essence.
- **TH:** I am guided by my higher self.

Quick Reference: Tapping Script Template

For a detailed guide, see Section 2.4, "Personalizing Your EFT Practice."

Title of Your Script: *(Descriptive title)*_____

Objective: *(Goal or intention)*_____

Setup Statement: *(While tapping on the Karate Chop point)*

"Even though I feel [specific emotion], I deeply and completely accept myself."

_____

_____

_____

Tapping Points and Reminder Phrases: *(Short reminder phrases for each point)*

EB: *"[Emotion or issue]"*_____

SE: *"[Emotion or issue]"*_____

UE: *"[Emotion or issue]"*_____

UN: *"[Emotion or issue]"*_____

CH: *"[Emotion or issue]"*_____

CB: *"[Emotion or issue]"*_____

UA: *"[Emotion or issue]"*_____

TH: *"[Emotion or issue]"*_____

Closing Statement:

_____

References

Andrade, J., Feinstein, D., & Wainstein, E. (2023). Randomized controlled trials of emotional freedom techniques: A review. *Journal of Evidence-Based Integrative Medicine, 28,* 36438382. https://pubmed.ncbi.nlm.nih.gov/36438382/

Bach, D., Groesbeck, G., Stapleton, P., Sims, R., Blickheuser, K., & Church, D. (2019). Clinical EFT (Emotional Freedom Techniques) improves multiple physiological markers of health. *Journal of Evidence-Based Integrative Medicine, 24,* 2515690X18823691. doi:10.1177/2515690X18823691

Benfield, J. (2023). Emotional freedom techniques (EFT): What it is and how it works. *Healthline.* https://www.healthline.com/health/eft-tapping#:~:text=Similar%20to%20acupuncture,%20EFT%20focuses,or%20emotion%20may%20have%20caused

Church, D., Yount, G., & Brooks, A. J. (2012). The effect of emotional freedom techniques on stress biochemistry: A randomized controlled trial. *Journal of Nervous and Mental Disease, 200*(10), 891-896. doi:10.1097/NMD.0b013e31826b9fc1

Church, D., Yount, G., Rachlin, K., Fox, L., & Nelms, J. (2016). Epigenetic effects of PTSD remediation in veterans using Clinical EFT (Emotional Freedom Techniques): A randomized controlled pilot study. *American Journal of Health Promotion, 1-11.* doi:10.1177/0890117116666115 4

Church, D., Stapleton, P., Sheppard, L., & Carter, B. (2018). Naturally thin you: Weight loss and psychological symptoms after a six-week online Clinical EFT (Emotional Freedom Techniques) course. *Explore (NY), 14*(2), 131-136. doi:10.1016/j.explore.2017.10.009

Clond, M. (2016). Emotional freedom techniques for anxiety: A systematic review with meta-analysis. *Journal of Nervous and Mental Disease, 204*(5), 388-395. https://www.ncbi.nlm.nih.gov/pmc/articles/PMC6381429/

Frontiers in Psychology. (2022, November 9). Psychology for clinical settings. *Frontiers in Psychology, 13*. https://doi.org/10.3389/fpsyg.2022.951451

Gratefulness.me. (2023). How to write affirmations: How to do affirmations. *Gratefulness Blog*. https://blog.gratefulness.me/how-to-write-affirmations-how-to-do-affirmations/

Live Your Truth. (2023). EFT tapping for emotional healing. *Carol Tuttle*. https://ct.liveyourtruth.com/eft-tapping-for-emotional-healing/

OpenAI. (2024). ChatGPT: An AI language model. Retrieved from https://www.openai.com/research/chatgpt

Ortner, N. (2023). The power of tapping for weight loss: A research review. *The Tapping Solution*. https://www.thetappingsolution.com/blog/the-power-of-tapping-for-weight-loss-a-research-review/

Purdue University. (2023). Emotional freedom technique: Research supports benefits of tapping for mental health. *Purdue Today*. https://www.purdue.edu/newsroom/purduetoday/releases/2023/Q3/emotional-freedom-technique-research-supports-benefits-of-tapping-for-mental-health.html

Stapleton, P., Chatwin, H., Sheppard, L., & McSawn, J. (2016). The lived experience of chronic pain and the impact of brief emotional freedom techniques (EFT) group therapy on coping. *Energy Psychology: Theory, Research, and Treatment, 8*(2), 18-28.

Stapleton, P., Crighton, G., Sabot, D., & O'Neill, H. M. (2020). Reexamining the effect of emotional freedom techniques on stress biochemistry:

A randomized controlled trial. *Psychological Trauma, 12*(8), 869-877. doi:10.1037/tra0000563

Stapleton, P., Sheldon, T., & Porter, B. (2012). Clinical benefits of emotional freedom techniques on food cravings at 12-months follow-up: A randomized controlled trial. *Energy Psychology Journal, 4*(1), 13-24.

Vitality Living College. (2023). How to use EFT on physical pain. *Vitality Living College.* https://vitalitylivingcollege.info/how-to-use-eft-on-physical-pain/

EFT Universe. (2023). EFT success stories. *EFT Universe.* https://eftuniverse.com/stories/

Chakra Boosters. (2023). EFT to integrate chakras. *Chakra Boosters.* https://www.chakraboosters.com/eft-to-integrate-chakras